Thought Models for Leadership

Use the mental techniques of the world´s greatest and richest to make better decisions, improve your career trajectory and gain more respect at work

By

Jonatan Slane

© Copyright 2019 - All rights reserved.

The content contained within this book may not be reproduced, duplicated or transmitted without direct written permission from the author or the publisher.
Under no circumstances will any blame or legal responsibility be held against the publisher, or author, for any damages, reparation, or monetary loss due to the information contained within this book. Either directly or indirectly.

Legal Notice:
This book is copyright protected. This book is only for personal use. You cannot amend, distribute, sell, use, quote or paraphrase any part, or the content within this book, without the consent of the author or publisher.

Disclaimer Notice:
Please note the information contained within this document is for educational and

entertainment purposes only. All effort has been executed to present accurate, up to date, and reliable, complete information. No warranties of any kind are declared or implied. Readers acknowledge that the author is not engaging in the rendering of legal, financial, medical or professional advice. The content within this book has been derived from various sources. Please consult a licensed professional before attempting any techniques outlined in this book.

By reading this document, the reader agrees that under no circumstances is the author responsible for any losses, direct or indirect, which are incurred as a result of the use of the information contained within this document, including, but not limited to, — errors, omissions, or inaccuracies.

Hello,

You live in a stressful and fast-paced business world.

As a leader you´re always looking to get the most out of your time and money.

When reading, everything seems logical and clear, but when you´re at work, you tend what to forget what you have read last month and move on as usual.

I have found a practical solution for you. One which doesn´t require any mental energy.

The book contains **38 thought models use by the world´s greatest and richest leaders**.

But you don´t change by just reading. Only concepts that you practice, and repeat will make it to your long-term memory.

So, my advice is to print these mental models. Tape the model you want to internalize to your computer screen or on your bathroom mirror. Put the model in your eyesight, so you´ll see it daily. This will help you to make higher quality and more rational decisions.

So, start using the Thought Models of successful leaders

Go to:

http://thoughtmodelsformen.businessleadershipplatform.com/

OR Scan the QR Code below

- Get the 38 models
- print the model you want to work on.
- start reading and initiate the desired change

Tip: **One model at a time.**

Enjoy the book.

Jonatan Slane

Business Leadership Platform

Table of Contents

Introduction — 11

Chapter 1 – Why We Use Models? — 21

   Simplify Things to Make a Better Impact — 33

   Omit Hidden Dimensions for the Betterment of Your Problem Solving — 35

   Be Realistic by Using Multidisciplinary Approaches — 37

   What You Do is Who You Are — 38

   This is What You Need — 39

   Mental Models at Work: The billionaire who made it! — 40

Chapter 2 – You Want to be Right — 47

   Confirmation Bias — 48

   The Reality About Maps — 50

   The Map and the Territory — 51

   Selective Perception — 60

   Ideology — 66

   Framing — 68

For Your Application... 73

Chapter 3 – Answering All These Questions 79

Mental Model #1: The First Principles 85

Mental Model #2: The Thought Experiment 92

Mental Model #3: The Second-Order Thinking 100

Mental Model #4: The Probabilistic Thinking 104

Mental Model #5: The Inversion Principle 106

Mental Model #6: The Loss Aversion/Fairness/Endowment Effect 108

Mental Model #7: The Sunk Costs/Commitment + Consistency Bias 112

Mental Model #8: Product vs. Packaging/Action Bias 115

Mental Model #9: The Base Rates 119

For Your Application... 121

Chapter 4 – Optimizing and Systemizing Productivity 125

1. Dealing with Stress 126

2. Be Highly Concerned About Mental Health 133

3. More Mental Models to Make Effective Decisions 138

Chapter 5 – Negotiation and How to Make it a Win-Win 177

Robert Cialdini and the Influence: The Psychology of Persuasion 180

Conclusion 203

References 209

Introduction

Lately, my colleagues and I were talking about the things that we usually see on social media like on Facebook, Twitter, Instagram, and even in Google News! We have a wide variety of topics that are very prominent on Facebook starting from current events, weather forecasts, historical flashbacks, down to funny trivial ones that didn't concern us at all. Aside from those topics, we were discussing our own lives and realizations as we age. Getting older each day gave us a panic attack that we talked about things that we don't usually get into the discussion. I am with my friends and colleagues for some years now and that made us bonded and comfortable with each other's presence. Recently, we had been asking each one, where we are right now? What we already achieved? Are we satisfied with what we have? Where are we heading?

Now, it seems unbelievable that the officemates and friends that I used to be drunk with and who didn't have time for serious group discussions because they were a bit awkward are already having a gradual change in their perspectives in life. That literally left me amazed and flabbergasted, just like what is totally happening to me. Nowadays, we are very much interested in talking about the security of our future, how to invest smartly, how we spend quality time with our families, how we can maintain a good healthy lifestyle. how to deal with toxic people, and other things that can cause us stress and anxiety. We can say that we are taking our maturity to a higher level.

To attain the mentality that we currently have today and to achieve the change or security that we want to happen in our lives means that we are learning not to repeat the mistakes that we had committed when we were younger. We must learn from our mistakes and rise from the ashes of our failures to have positive patterns that are affecting our growth. We learned from the repeated mistakes brought by an impulse that are constantly pestering our peers and other people around us. We have learned to observe recurring events and to perceive new concepts that are becoming *mental models* that we are looking at. Yes, we have **mental models** that are repeating ideas that gave us mental images of scenarios, which become a *model* that we can utilize in similar circumstances. These models are very powerful tools that are not universally acquired at any academic level. You can possess mental models through practical life experiences, reading other individuals' practices, and your own observation in life.

You might be using mental models without being fully aware that you are actually applying one. So, this book is good for you so you can learn more about mental models that can help you become a more effective decision-maker. Even I, earlier in my life, was not aware that I was already using mental models. By listening to other people's suggestions on how to fix my problems, I was able to use the mental models that were proven effective for them. That is one example of a mental model, when you listen to other people's experiences and how they managed to solve problems effectively. For us, social validation is essential so we can save time, energy, and effort in solving problems. Furthermore, it is a normal reaction to be disappointed if the outcome doesn't go the way we wanted it to be. That's when we rely on our own or, we will try another way until we solve the problem. In this process of trial and error, we are collecting mental models and we discriminate if one model or combination of it would be effective in solving one situation.

Also, in this book, you will learn different mental models that you can apply in situations personally and at work. Every day, we are making decisions that can be right or wrong; decisions that will surely affect the future and the variables in our surroundings. You will meet toxic people and unexpected circumstances that will surely challenge your patience. In my experience, I have been supervising the newly hired employees in the company I am working at. Being a mentor at the beginning was like a blessing and a curse at the same time. To nurture the minds and develop the skills of the trainees that I was handling gave me fulfillment. I said that I found the purpose of staying in a career that I was starting to dislike. Then, my struggles started when some of my haters started to question my capabilities as the newly appointed trainer. I was appointed after I celebrated my first-year anniversary. The pressure became heavier when my trainees violated some of the basic company rules. Since I wasn't trained as a trainer, it allowed me to create my own techniques and I started to follow my instinct. I prepared my own training materials, formulated my own topic syllabus, reinvented myself during discussions and formed my own way of instilling disciplines among my trainees. Every time that I was discussing at the training room, I felt like I was the master of my own universe. I got addicted to the adoration of my trainees. And the saddest part of all, I took advantage of the little authority that I had once. Until one day, everyone in the office seemed to hate me and even my closest allies were abandoning me.

I can say that I decided to teach to help a company and it is also my decision to be eaten by work and superiority. The most important lesson I learned is always to be down-to-earth and do not forget the people who helped you when you are still a nobody. I deserved all the wraths of the people around me. That was when I decided to change, and I reached out with the people who were always there when I need them the most. When I was abusing my authority, I was always depressed and there was no happiness in my heart. I was very impulsive with the stupidity of others. I tried to be a better version of myself and begun my holistic rehabilitation. I had to keep myself low and extended the boundaries of my understanding.

My collection of mental models helped me to be a better version of myself and I won the support of my friends and colleagues again. I have proven that mental models helped me always to look back and to remember the person that I was once.

I know that you are dealing with problems and you want to have the best decision to apply in all of your difficulties. I do understand your needs personally and professionally. I want to expose you more about how mental models will help you achieve the success that you want in your life. Mental models can also help you gain the income that you are dreaming of. Further in this book, you will get to know successful individuals who relied heavily on mental models and how they became billionaires, speakers, authors, and inspirations to people around the globe who always wanted to achieve what successful people have accomplished. I had cited Charles Munger, a self-made billionaire, who has deep wisdom about mental models because of his expertise in many disciplines and you will learn about his techniques as you dive into the pages of this book. I learned a lot from that guy, and I am sure that you will also idolize the partner of the famous investor, Warren Buffett.

Life has many chances and mysteries to offer you. All you have to do, in order to have a peaceful and successful life is to build your own personal concepts by learning by the experiences of those people who knew a deeper secret regarding their existence. With this book, I can give you a glimpse of how people become successful and attain a meaningful lifestyle by utilizing mental models and applied them to be effective decision-makers.

I believe that after you read this book, you will be capable of collecting your own toolbox loaded with powerful mental models that you can apply to various challenging situations. I am looking forward to helping you produce successful decisions that will benefit not just you, but all the people around you and your environment as well. Upon learning the fundamentals of mental models, you can also teach their concepts to your family, friends, or anybody else. You can bring positive change to yourself while sharing the gospel of mental models.

Now, I want you to find a comfortable place... where you can absorb everything that is written in this book. Gather yourself together, muster your energy, and go deep into concentration as you dive inside the wonders of this book. I will join you in a new realm where mental models and their proponents give reality to the success you've been seeking.

Chapter 1 – Why We Use Models?

Television and social media are highly regarded as the fastest and effective way to advertise products and disseminate information. The most common effect that they can build to everyone is how people perceive things with multiple facets or definitions. Like for example, when we talk about models most people would agree that the term is used to describe people whose faces are printed in magazines. Those people who are walking on runways, or it can be device prototypes. These definitions are correct. But what we are going to discuss in this book is a way deeper and helpful to professionals and other working individuals.

Models are very important when you actually want to attain a specific goal. For example, education starts at home and parents are the first teachers who guided us to gain good manners and right conduct. I can still remember when I was young, and my mother was lecturing me about giving to the poor and sharing what little I have to other children who were in need. She used to tell stories about the generosity and selflessness of Mother Theresa who was elevated to sainthood in 2016. Until today, the heroic deeds of Mother Theresa still linger in my memory and I even shared her stories to children whenever I have the chance to act as a volunteer teacher in one of the organizations that I am actively participating in. My mother recounted Saint Theresa and used her as a factual model to effectively instill to my brain the importance of sharing. Surely, your parents had used superheroes, biblical characters, or other prominent figures in history that have impacted the persons that we are today. Different kinds of models have also been utilized in different fields for the advancement of humanity. Theoretical models are used in business industries to maximize profits and to sustain the global economy. There are also different infrastructures in the field of information technology (IT) that continuously evolve like the emergence of artificial intelligence. Even regular people are following models that govern their day-to-day existence. There are essential models that are innately part of humanity and we call them ***mental models***.

If you haven't heard about a mental model, it simply explains how a thing works and it is a recurring concept. It is also a label for any kind of perception or concept that we carry in our minds. Mental models are very vital because they help us understand the essence of life and make the way we live much easier. Game theory is among the popular mental models because its fundamental purpose is understanding the importance of trust and relationships. Mental models are vital gears for knowledge compilation, and they create a wide base of information. Our knowledge starts with grain and it keeps expanding as we get older and earn more experiences. When we find missing pieces or gaps between parts in our information base, we tend to find and add new pieces to form a connection that would fill out those gaps. With mental models, you can have a better approach when dealing with problems. By identifying where you are effective and good at, you can start right there and think of strategies that would solve the problem partially or the whole of it.

Decision-making is a tough job that every one of us is undertaking and there are situations where we need to choose and weigh in carefully our options to select the best solution. Mental models are relevant in decision making because they mostly led to success when properly executed. But it doesn't mean that having a mental model will always end up successfully. There are moments that following a specific mental model brings a person to fail. When a person is weak at making decisions, failure means that another mental model should be used or even change that person's setting to save his face. I want you to instill in your mind that even failures can pave the way to a much better opportunity. I think it is important for me to tackle the factors that make a decision.

Smashing Magazine published an article in February 2019 on how people usually make decisions.[1] Emotions play an important factor in decision-making and most decisions are not logically planned because emotions interfere. Most decisions are also made unconsciously. There are researchers who observed brain activity and they could successfully predict what decision people would do within 7-10 seconds before they even realize what they made as a decision.[2] It means, even when we think that we are making a logical and conscious decision, there are still chances that we are not really aware that we already made a decision unconsciously and its implication to others and to the environment. When we are in fear and doubtful, we always choose decisions that are safe enough to avoid conflicts. It is a major problem in decision-making if you can't feel emotions and if you can't also empathize with other people. Our instinct depends on what we feel. Let us go a bit scientific. There is this specific part of the brain that regulates fear and that is the *ventromedial prefrontal cortex* (vmPFC). Other parts of the brain, like the amygdala in particular where conditioned fear reactions are created, tell us when to be afraid and what to be afraid of while vmPFC is opposing the conditioned fear and stops a person from being afraid in certain scenarios. When vmPFC is active, a person can ignore conditioned fears that enable decision making. To make an effective decision, you need to admit that emotions are necessary and play an important factor in planning. Instead of focusing on logical arguments for validation, you are more likely to produce wise and effective decisions by understanding situations and be more empathic if there are other people involved. According to studies, there is a specific kind of neuron that travels into the brain that allows people to act when the brain is confident enough of a decision. It is more likely based on instinct that made this matter subjective once a decision is not based on the data collected but a product of mere confidence.[2]

In fact, the outcomes of a certain decision are unpredictable. No matter how logically accurate your data are, there might be unexpected or unpredicted factors that affect our decisions, causing them to fail big time. I know that just like me, you had experienced making a decision which turned out opposite to what you were expecting. It was a very common reaction to explain why it failed and to regret it afterward.

Let us take the case of the war between Spain and England in the 16th century. Spain and England dominated the European political arena during the second half of the sixteenth century. Spain was ruled by the prudent Catholic king, Philip II; while England was ruled by the Protestant and virgin queen, Elizabeth I. King

Philip and Queen Elizabeth were siblings-in-law because Queen Mary was Philip's wife and half-sister of Elizabeth. Upon the death of Queen Mary who was the ruler of England for five short years, Elizabeth ascended to power. Papal authority was a prominent force during this era and since Elizabeth was a Protestant, with one wrong move, she could earn an excommunication. Protestantism was still young at the time and Elizabeth was the ultimate champion of the newly established religion and she supported Protestant allies, an act that was distasteful for the Roman Catholic Church. Elizabeth was poised to be excommunicated but Philip protected Elizabeth at all costs from the Papal wrath. Philip was helping Elizabeth because he wanted to marry her for political alliance and to put England back to Catholicism. Until Elizabeth begun to support the Dutch against Spain, military intervention in the Netherlands, the beheading of the Catholic Queen Mary of Scots, and the ambush of English pirates against Spanish ships tolerated by

Elizabeth were the major factors for the launching of the Spanish Armada in 1588.[3] This so-called invincible Armada was consisted of 130 ships that carried 2,500 guns, 8,000 seamen, and 20,000 soldiers. Such a figure worried Elizabeth and her subjects that they relied heavily on divine intervention.[4] The heavens seemed to smile at England because many ships of the approaching Armada were ruined by the storm. The exhausted Armada was confronted by the waiting English naval fleet to protect the boundaries of the English coast. Obviously, the Armada outnumbered the English forces but because of the raging storm, the Armada's ships decreased and left the other ships damaged. Elizabeth had brilliant naval officers that led the English to win the war. The Armada lost at sea and it was among the most humiliating defeat in Spanish naval history while England entered a golden age and became the Empress of the Seas governed by the pure Queen Elizabeth.

With Spain's wealth and military might, it can crash England easily. Sending too many soldiers carried by gigantic ships brought fear to Elizabeth. But there were unexpected circumstances that made it possible for England to win the war like the storms that injured the Spanish Armada and the experienced English officials who made effective tactics that destroyed their enemies. Yes, King Philip regretted his decision because being defeated by Queen Elizabeth weaken his popularity and increased the latter's capacity to rule. Well, nobody wants to experience a war and to see one country beaten by another one. King Philip by that time thought that launching his Armada in 1588 was the best time to oppose Elizabeth and to completely restore Catholicism in England.

Success is sweet and is always attributed to good decision making while failure is constantly explained by bad decisions and a series of bad luck. In my experience, good decisions can also lead to failure as well and vice versa. Decision-making is like your gambling because data and other factors might be helpful, but you are not sure where it will lead you. That's why it is a normal reaction while making a decision to ask yourself the possible outcomes of your options. For Darius Foroux, that is an incomprehensive method not to question the decision-making process because you are more likely looking at the possible outcome.[5] That is why mental models are important because it is your thinking mechanism about how you perceive things. There are times that we tend to skip the process and decided right away, and several factors might include a lack of resources, familiarity, or time. To bypass a decision-making process makes a person a bad decision-maker. You have to focus on how comprehensive your process is rather than focusing on the success rate of your choices. In fact, you don't need to know all about mental models. All you just have to do is to internalize the fundamental core and find models that are effective for you and for situations that you need to apply mental models.

Do not be like other professionals who speak about mental models but lack the system of application to achieve meaningful goals. Always remember that knowledge without even applying it is useless at all. We cannot see the future accurately because we are not psychics, nor even understand all the mental models. By studying and applying a comprehensive thinking process, it can give us satisfaction no matter what the outcome is. And in that way, we can avoid any forms of regret that might hurt as deeply. Inaction is a kind of regret that can literally make you unhappy. Always keep in mind that mistakes are lessons that make us better individuals.

There are countless possibilities in our world and uncertainty is just around the corner. With mental models, they help us to reduce some doubts about our decisions. Now, we will dissect how mental models enable you to become smarter and effective decision-maker.[6]

Simplify Things to Make a Better Impact

There are too many things in our lives that we take for granted. There are times that we are very inconsiderate about the fact that what happens to us is created by countless possibilities brought by different phenomena that are pulled together to yield a certain product. What we see initially is just something on the surface and not the outcome beneath it. If you have the power to manipulate or to play the things that directly affect the outcome, then you might bring it on your side to produce the result you want. The question is, how would you identify the variables to play along with?

It is like suicide if you will try to influence everything and be disappointed with the result. That's when you use mental models to give you the full potential to filter unnecessary elements and improve your decisions. To give you an example, we have this famous topic in statistics known as Pareto's Principle which is known as the power law. This principle states that a very little portion of essential variables has more of an impact on the outcome than all of the rest combined. The billionaires Charlie Munger and his partner, Warren Buffett, used this principle when they are making investment decisions. They don't buy stock without undergoing their system that evaluates if a certain company is undervalued or not relevant to any industry. They are thoroughly looking for potentials from small stuff that will produce massive profits. When you study their corporate records, most of their earnings came from a very little section. By being highly aware of the model you are using, you can utilize it in other situations where your sole judgment is put to the test. It provides you a strainer to filter the most important variables to work and focus on and which ones to disregard. Other models have different outlines that can be used to determine correct and important details.

Mental models do difficult tasks on our behalf and they help us to simplify intricacy.

Omit Hidden Dimensions for the Betterment of Your Problem Solving

The human mind is very fast to discriminate and to establish cause and effect which can be considered as the brain's strengths and weaknesses. We are more likely to be blinded by the initial result rather than looking at a deeper level. Yet, this factor is actually a mental model because it allows us to sort things to make sense out of everything and it gives us an easier way of understanding our environment. Somehow, it also permits us to take shortcuts in learning new things. And that is also when it becomes bad because what we are connecting with is often wrong.

Charles Munger loves and an advocate of the idea that it is better to minimize shortcomings by evading errors than it is to be perfect. According to Munger, if you are doing things that are exposing you to destruction, your luck will be exhausted no matter how brilliant you are. As humans, we have innate blind spots that expose us to harm. Behavioral economics states that we don't comprehend our surroundings rationally because we have different kinds of biases which are more potent than the way we think. By using mental models, we are making ourselves aware of those biases and think a way better. Also, because of these biases, once it becomes evident in a situation, we can think twice or more before making a decision. By formulating a checklist that will help you find the right mental models when making big choices, you are significantly reducing the possibility of losing and committing mistakes.

Be Realistic by Using Multidisciplinary Approaches

Charles Munger became a wealthy and very successful person because of his habit of collecting diverse mental models. It seems that he believes in the idea that the whole is greater than the sum of its parts, or that two are always better than one. Munger famously quoted that it is best to have multiple models since the human psychology is so powerful that you have the ***capacity to torture reality so that it fits your model.*** He is exerting that you must not give up trying until you get the very fruit of your labor. These models have to originate from multiple disciplines because of the very fact that all the wisdom that exists in this world is not found in just one academic faculty.

What You Do is Who You Are

What we practice in our career tells us who we are or what we specialized in. A businessperson is inclined to evaluate decisions using disciplines that have planted in his mind at work while a scientist and a researcher are relying on experiments and hypotheses. If you see, they have limited frameworks that they can use to discriminate before coming up with a final decision. The world offers so many dimensions other than what we learned through our existence. For your mental models to be effective, they must be proven and compete with others by attacking different situations. Always assume that individual models are somewhat wrong, but a good collection combined can mitigate and filter these errors and pave the way to a winning decision.

You don't have to be an expert in every discipline. Because mastering them requires energy and a great amount of intelligence.

Attempting to master every discipline might leave you insane. You just have to understand the fundamentals of many disciplines and use them to make decisions in your everyday life.

This is What You Need

There are many of us who are trying to use status to dictate the factors of existence. The higher the income, the more entitled others are projecting themselves. That is a very limited way of living, and it is also damaging to one's image, reputation, and pursuit of life. Let us take another look at Charlie Munger who is typically shy under the media's presence. But when he opens his mouth to deliver his speech, his audience listens because what he shares is valuable. His deep knowledge and practical application of mental models offer a remarkable tool in decision-making and problem-solving. There are countless ways to get and to utilize mental models to improve our lives. You can always use notes, reminders, checklist, and raise consciousness about mental models.

Mental Models at Work: The billionaire who made it!

Mental models are really powerful tools that can lead you to success and can give you access to a much more meaningful life. There are many moguls in different parts of the world who dominated their corresponding fields of expertise because they use mental models effectively. So effective and helpful that they suggested their mental models whenever they were invited for an interview or during their public speeches. The best examples who used mental models are the billionaires Charlie Munger and his partner, Warren Buffet. Let us take a ride and explore the mental models Charlie Munger, a self-made billionaire, who used effectively to be a successful man that he is today.

Charlie Munger, also famously known by his nickname Charlie, is considered to be one of the great minds of the 20th century. He is currently the vice-chairman of Berkshire Hathaway Corp., owned by a famous investor named Warren Buffett. Munger is also the chairman of the Daily Journal in Los Angeles. He is the director of Costco Wholesale Corp. He is a longtime resident of Pasadena in California and he was born in Omaha, Nebraska in 1924. During his teenage years, he worked at Buffett & Son, a grocery store owned by the grandfather of his future business partner, Warren Buffett.[7] He studied Mathematics in the University of Michigan but eventually dropped out a few days after his 19th birthday to enter in the United States Army Air Corps where he served as a second lieutenant. He then continued college studying meteorology at Caltech in California. His curiosity and thirst for knowledge led him to take advanced courses in several universities including Harvard University where he completed law school. He graduated as *magna cum laude* with a J.D. in Harvard Law School in 1948 and he was a part of the Harvard Legal Aid Bureau.

Munger founded and served as a real state attorney at Munger, Tolles & Olson in 1962 which is currently a prominent law firm. He concentrated on investments, he gave up practicing law and partnered with Otis Booth in real estate development. Munger is highly associated with his business partner, Warren Buffett, whom he met in 1959 and formed an investment relationship. As per Buffet's essay entitled *The Superinvestors of Graham-and-Doddsville* published in 1984, from 1962 to 1975, Munger operated his own investment partnership that generated compound annual returns of 19.8%.

Munger's success in the field of law and financial investment made him a self-made billionaire and inspired millions of people across the globe.

His groundbreaking methods in achieving a winning life prompted different universities, organizations, and organizers to invite him as a speaker in their seminars and other functions. His speeches, as well as his best-selling book Poor Charlie's Almanack, introduced the model of **elementary, worldly wisdom** which also relates to the field of business and finance. Munger believed that high ethical standards are vital to his principles of success.

Through the years, Munger developed a comprehensive system of **multiple mental models** and thanks for his love of academics that he was able to attain his dreams. His reinvention through his commitment to studying different fields aside from law and business include psychology, economics, physics, biology, and history. His mental models made him capable of having an accurate solution to complex problems. His viewpoint about career and life is very rare, accurate, and standout with surprising reliability. This method is called by many as the **Munger approach** which is difficult. But once you undertake and understand its fundamental code of belief, it will help you to wipe out the uncertainties in your mind easily. Munger once shared the secret to his success and it is simply because he is a rational being who applies rational and attainable solutions.

Munger is typically shy and doesn't want to be pestered by the media until he gave his very famous speech in 1994 at USC Business School and ushered the world to the general framework about making wise decisions. He and Buffett are learning machines, a fact that made them successful and produced billions of dollars in profit. They are collecting mental models on how the world works and utilize what they learned to solve every problem in different ways before having the best final solution. As the famous proverb says, *two heads are better than one*. One mental model alone is not entirely perfect and effective, but with a good collection permit us to see everything around us from a better angle.

Charles Munger is really an inspiration and an idol to look up to. His mental models allow him to have an optimistic vista of the world and its components. He made the best decisions especially in the field of business that made him a sought-after investor and team player. His assets provided for him and even his philanthropic works which are helping many people and organizations in great needs.

Chapter 2 – You Want to be Right

The advent of technology has brought significant development in the field of biology. Nowadays, people who wanted to modify their body parts can consult plastic surgeons and undergo expensive procedures to be desirable and for the sake of aesthetics. Imagine that you have been riding on the elevator, going down to the lobby, you have seen a person with radiant skin, a pair of healthy breasts, long attractive legs, long straight hair, and wearing a revealing red cocktail dress. Of course, what you have witnessed is a perfect example of a lady, a naturally born to the female species. You were mesmerized by what you saw. You stepped out from the elevator and went out to grab a taxi. Back in the elevator, the lady that you have encountered went back to her room to get an identification card that will be used on some errands. The name that was written on the card is SMITH, MARK W. Mark Smith who just completed his gender reassignment operation. Mark is still currently in the process of healing and is on the way to meet his lawyer to take legal actions on changing his name and gender and be identified as a transsexual woman. A situation like this is a good example of *"What we see is what we get"*. It is, of course, easy to believe in the evidence and with your intuition, jump into the conclusion that you have seen a natural woman. You believe in what you saw without further validation and you are convinced that his persona as a natural woman is true. That is very dangerous if we believe instantly to something that we have just seen. This is an example of ***confirmation bias***.

Confirmation Bias

According to Psychology Today, confirmation bias happens to start from the direct influence of desire on what we believe.[1] It can also be defined as the tendency to collect and interpret new data in a biased way to validate preexisting principles. Another example is when people still stick to obsolete theories in the presence of apparently obvious evidence. When we want a certain concept or thought to exist, we end up believing that it is true. Therefore, we are being inspired by wishful thinking, or else, false hope. This mistake leads some of us to stop collecting data when the variables gathered, in the long run, validate the views or prejudgments that we desire to be real. The moment that we have created an image, we are gladly embracing the information confirming that what we believed is authentic and correct. Doing this process allows you to reject or to ignore evidence which contradicts your own established facts. Confirmation bias also suggests that we don't see situations objectively. We gather bits of information that make us happy due to the fact that it confirms our belief. Sad to say but in reality, it makes us prisoners of our own assumptions.

The Reality About Maps

A map is a very useful tool in humankind. According to Merriam-Webster, a map is a representation that is usually on a flat surface of the whole or just a part of an area.[2] A map also emphasizes relationships between variables of various space-like objects, places, or themes. They are very helpful for navigators and other professionals who work with maps. Just like everything that exists in this world, maps are imperfect. They are flawed and yet very vital. They are replicas of reality, and as replicas, they are reductions of their reference. Maps don't have the exact qualities or attributes of what they are portraying. Maps are no longer useful to humanity if they were to represent things with perfect symmetry or they are no less than a reduction of the real object.

The Map and the Territory

Alfred Korzybski was born on July 3, 1879, in Warsaw, Poland in an aristocratic family known to produce several scientists and mathematicians for generations.[2] He studied engineering at Warsaw University of Technology. Later, he entered the Second Russian Army during World War I as a volunteer and served as an intelligence officer. His service brought him serious internal injuries and badly wounded his legs. After the war, he decided to stay in the United States where he continued his academic endeavors. The first-ever world war is an ugly part of history which brought a deep impact to Korzybski and he questioned why people involved in such catastrophic and senseless actions. This prompted him to compare human behavior to animal behavior to find the differences. Such a venture allowed him to publish his first book in 1921 entitled *Manhood of Humanity: The Science of Human Engineering*. It was a success and he ventured in the field of psychiatry. Korzybski is famously known for giving birth to the field of general semantics that is a philosophical approach to language. Its formulation seeks to navigate the connection between the totality of language, its function, and efforts to stimulate an individual's capability to express thoughts.

Korzybski presented a paper on mathematical semantics in 1931 in New Orleans, Louisiana. For a layperson and a non-technical reader, the mathematician's arguments on the connection of mathematics to human language, and to reality are difficult to comprehend and unnecessary. But Korzybski's string of ideas on the formation of language promoted his concept that ***the map is not the territory.*** Meaning to say, the usual description of an object is not the object itself. That the model is not authentic and not even the reality. That is abstracted is not abstracted. According to Korzybski:

A map may contain a formation that is the same or not to the formation of the place.

1. Two identical structures have identical *logical* features. Therefore, if you apply it in a correct map, Dresden is provided between Paris and Warsaw and an identical connection is available in the actual place.
2. A map is not a definite territory.
3. A perfect map must contain the map of the map and its map, and so on. This characteristic can be called **self-reflexiveness**.

Maps are very important, but they are imperfect. In this context, maps are a representation of the concept of what is real that includes explanations, philosophies, prototypes, and the like. To fully understand the map, we need to have an abstraction or a definite concept that will guide us to solve our problems. We always have to admit reality. In order to solve any problem, our minds produce maps of reality to better understand and interpret the situation due to the fact that the effective way we can identify the difficulty of reality is by abstraction.

53

Most of the time, we don't understand our own maps and what their limits are. In reality, we are so clingy on the abstraction that we are accustomed to utilizing inappropriate models and patterns because we often believe in the idea that it is better to use *any* preference than *none at all*. An example of such a dilemma can be found in the workplace. I have a colleague who had confessed the craziest step he did so far in completing a project on time. He used to submit things on time or earlier than due. Then, there was this project that would have been completed ahead of time if updates were applied and saved correctly. My colleague was very busy and there came an incident that made him cram until the next day. His computer went dead for several minutes because the person sitting in front of his station triggered an unknown peripheral that turned off his computer. He was problematic because he didn't save the edits he applied so, he started to repeat the process. Adrenaline rush came in and since it was the project's due, he decided to send an incomplete file. Feedback is usually given a day or two. So in case the client notices that the project is not yet done, my colleague would tell me that he sent the wrong file and the updated version will be sent right away. Or, since he was confident that he would finish the project the next day, he will tell the client that he sent the wrong file and then will upload the completed version of the file. What happened was the latter, he emailed the client and the client responded nicely. What my colleague did was a bit risky because the client could have reacted differently. He can tell the truth, but he decided to compromise his image, with the name of the company stipulated on him. He was really lucky at that time because the client was very polite.

Even the most prominent and accurate maps have limitations. According to Korzybski, some of their limitations are: they could be wrong without us noticing it; maps are a reduction of the actual model that loses vital information and they need a scientific interpretation that usually causes major errors. With the groundbreaking discoveries in modern psychology, another issue has been raised about the human brain: it takes vast leaps and detours to interpret and understand the environment. Charlie Munger once stated that a decent idea and the human mind work like the sperm and egg – that when the first good idea comes in, the passage seals. This possibility may cause major problems for the sake of simplifying reality. Once we try a certain model and it works, we tend to overuse it even to situations where it is not potent at all. We have the difficulty of categorizing it and its uses that often cause mistakes. Let us discuss another corporate sample.

Ron Johnson was a force to be reckoned with in his success to change the marketing strategy of Target from an elite department store to a quality-yet-affordable retail shop for all types of consumers by the late 1990s to early 2000s. His successful maneuver of the Target Corporation was not left unnoticed came into the knowledge of the late Steve Jobs, the famous CEO and co-founder of Apple, Inc. Johnson's success in building the Apple Stores into prominence was gradual and yet undeniable. According to the report released by Fortune Media in 2011, Apple Stores were the most productive worldwide on a per-square-foot basis and became a supreme force in the retail world.[3] Apple's sales put the famous jewelry store Tiffany's on the second spot. After taking charge of Apple's formidable position in the business world, Johnson was hired by other legends of the financial world including Steven Roth and Bill Ackman. His next task was to modernize the image of the old-fashioned department store chain JC Penney. The store was in a very dire situation and a transformation must be done. The retail market share consumed by department stores had declined from 57% to 31% between 1992 and 2001. Compared to other struggling retailers at that time, JC Penney was still making some considerable profit because it had a valuable real estate and mall positioning. Plus, the rent was cheaper compared to other retailers which were a major advantage. Therefore, JC Penney had enough money to fund its transformation.

Johnson applied the technique he did for Apple that included the best customer service, static pricing with no markups and markdowns, attractive displays and quality products. Johnson envisioned to convert the stores into tiny malls-within-malls. This approach would make JC Penney trendy and reestablished as a prime and competitive retailer. During corporate meetings, Johnson discussed his idea persuasively that led to the store's soaring stock price from $26 in the summer of 2011 to $42 in early 2012. But it didn't last long because of the failure of Johnson's new model which eliminated discounting. Consumers who relied heavily on discount coupons rebelled and most of the products on display were seen too chic. The transformation of JC Penney which is originally known for its affordable sweaters was not a hit for its loyal consumers as well as the general public. As a consequence, Johnson was later fired for the expensive transformation of JC Penney which caused millions of dollars of operating losses.

Here is the question. What went wrong to Johnson's approach to JC Penney? We cannot question Johnson's effectivity and competency as a strategist. Even if we forget his success in Target and Apple, he still managed to propel JC Penney's undervalued stocks for a short period of time. The problem is, the success was not sustained longer than expected and losses soon came after. Its regular customers were not pleased by the sudden transformation of JC Penney from a mid-range to a high-end, trendy store. Obviously, Johnson used the old map he used in his previous campaigns, was proven ineffective and it even ruined his reputation. He utilized a map that he no longer needed because JC Penney's situation was demanding for a new map to be explored. Johnson had a wonderful vision and promoted a strategic proposal about retailing that was compatible in some situations, but not applicable in anymore in other cases. The landscape had changed, but the sad part is there is no innovation because he was hooked and stuck in the same old idea.

Warren Buffet is a successful investor who is fond of taking risks. At the same time, he advocated the use of multiple mental models. As the founder and owner of Berkshire Hathaway, he ran it smoothly without relying on computer models because it consumes a lot of resources like space, cash, and manpower. For him, it is better to admit that he has no power to see the future and depend greatly on his practical experiences.

Selective Perception

The emergence of mobile phones in the late '90s is unstoppable, and it led to the product's continuous innovation up to this era.[4] From the simple capacity of sending messages and making calls, today, mobile phones are powerful enough to control appliances at home or to manage financial transactions. Thanks to the available technology and resources that made such visions possible. And speaking of phones, we always have our favorite brands and personal preferences when acquiring one. Some of my friends have iPhones, some are loyal to Huawei, and I put my trust in Samsung. When my friends asked me why I love Samsung, I explained the pros and cons. They reacted without interest and talked about their phone's capabilities and suggested me to change my brand. Of course, I won't change my brand because it works for me. In vice versa, when I asked my friends to change their brands, I got their smiles and they ignored my pitch no matter how hard I tried to convince them.

When our favorites are being subjected to scrutiny, we are defensive and protective. We reject any forms of criticism and ignore what others are saying. This perceptual process is what you call *selective perception*.

Selective perception

A method in which an individual only accepts his desires and sets aside other's methods or beliefs.[5] There are factors that could influence selective perception. Like us, our past experiences have a direct bearing on selective perception mechanisms. Seymour Smith is an advertising researcher who said that individuals embrace advertisement that conforms on their beliefs, attitudes, conditioning, preferences, and a lot more. Selective perception can also be affected by biological factors such as age, race, and gender. The most powerful factor that may affect selective perception is the person's emotional extent, needs and wants.

Perceptual vigilance and **perceptual defense** are the two types of selective perception. Perceptual vigilance is the lower degree of selective perception and it connects to the method wherein the person notices and realizes the stimuli that may be vital for him at some level. **Stimuli** are actions, conditions, or persons that provoke a response.[6] Perceptual defense, on the other hand, is a high degree. It happens when a person is trying to make a shield against the stimuli to be protected against acquiring knowledge of it. Commonly, these stimuli are known to be intimidating or disagreeable, like vulgar words and abominable actions. This level of selective perception often ignores the negative facts of the subject. Research shows that people with a high degree of perceptual defense tend to have a powerful perceptual wall that acts as a filter, allowing them not to perceive unpleasant stimuli.

Based on early research, when selective perception is done consciously, it may lead the person to have a sight of things he wants and ignore its opposite. The best example of this case is the classic research that included subjects from famous universities of Princeton and Dartmouth. Respondents from these universities were instructed to watch a recorded football game between the two. According to the result, respondents from Dartmouth noticed that Princeton accumulated too many violations compared to its opponent. While subjects from Princeton, on the contrary, noticed the Dartmouth had the most violations during the game. This case shows a selective perception of opposing teams.

Selective perception can be tested and many professionals during the early 21st century conducted experiments and research to amass information and understand more the concept of selective perception. The most well-known selective perception test was conducted in 1999 by two psychologists Daniel Simons and Christopher Chabris.[7] The test was called the ***Invisible Gorilla Test***. This test was filmed and to give you a glimpse of the said video, allow me to describe it to you.

There were six people and the three of them are wearing white shirts while the other half is wearing black. You will be instructed to focus and do a silent count of the number of passes the players in white shirts can make. In the middle, a gorilla appears in the focus of the camera as it thumps its chest and then goes away. You definitely saw the gorilla. But when the proponents of the experiment conducted the live test at Harvard University, half of the participants who were instructed to count the number of passes didn't notice the gorilla. They simply focused on the instruction and ignored the animal. Therefore, the experiment reveals two important things. One is that we are missing many things around us. The second is, we are not aware that we are already missing too much.[7] People can concentrate on a single stimulus or event and tend to be **blinded** to what is coming ahead unexpectedly. This effect is known as **intentional blindness**.

Ideology

There are things that we stand up for and we are trying our best to live the life that we are comfortable with. Ideology is the word globally utilized to define the fundamental values, ideas, beliefs and rules that mold the behavioral method to economic, cultural, political, and social norms of a person or a group. In a larger scope, there are worldwide ideologies like fascism, conservatism, socialism, Christianity, Buddhism, and the like. A common ideology, shared by people with the same goals and advocacy, frequently work together as one to achieve a significant and ideal social impact for a valuable outcome. Ideology roots during childhood that we start learning from people around us. At first, we are participants guided by older individuals like our parents, siblings, grandparents, etc. These people made us players in an event or activity wherein we were taught to copy or observe the responses and attitudes of the people around us. This is what we call

socialization. Also, during this childhood development of ideological schema, it is vital to recognize the ideological factors that will serve as our guide in the future. We tend to imitate our elders until we find our own imperatives that shaped the ideals that we are fighting for and to believe in something.

Our ideology allows us to filter every information that is coming to us and accept the best ones that fit our ideals and ignore the rest of those that are unnecessary.

Google is an Eden for IT professionals and business executives because of its in-demand and trendy services. Google knows how to value its clients as well as its employees. It offers a competitive salary, countless benefits, free food, flexible working hours, and a lot more. The best perk I've seen personally is your pet can tag along with you once you become an employee. Google's management believes that pets and other recreational activities, except substance abuse and gambling, during working hours help their employees to be more productive, creative, and responsible. I hope that every company around the globe has the same ideology as Google but of course, some work environments are too hostile and having pets and doing recreational activities during working hours can compromise productivity.

Framing

Our minds respond to the situation in which a thing is attached and not just to the object itself. Framing is a very vital function of our brain. It is one way to look for patterns in disorder. It is another way to form sense out of insignificance. Every day, we are subjected to the framing battle which is one of the basic difficulties we can encounter as we continue to exist. The events, things, experiences, methods, and facts we learned are the components that give meaning to reality. Reality is dynamic, contextual, and actively constructed. The building process includes choices that we want to apply in our experience. What we want to have in every experience is of great importance. The framing options that you select identify the value, essence, limitations, and design of your experience. The rules of framing can be actively controlled by different social players like organizations and people around you to impose their personal agenda. The best example can be observed in the political landscape where different factions are framing and fighting over issues that greatly interest the public. If the majority of people believed that marijuana affects the brain negatively, marijuana use would be seen as illegal.

Framing can disturb you in different ways. If back at work you feel unhappy and undervalued, what could be your problem? You can make your own version of reality by framing that you have hostile and narcissistic bosses and find a better one. Framing has been greatly studied in behavioral economics wherein Israeli-American psychologists Amos Tversky and Daniel Kahneman found how framing influences many dimensions of decision-making. When they observed how individuals work with the unknown, it was revealed that there were constant biases in the responses. These biases could be products of **heuristics** or **mental shortcuts**. Some of these shortcuts were very obvious and people are more likely to make inferences from their personal experiences. For instance, if you felt like you were not giving your best at work and you were not doing things right, you have the tendency to overestimate and see yourself unemployed anytime soon. Tversky and Kahneman conducted another experiment by asking their subjects to estimate the number of African nations that were members of the United Nations. They had a wheel of fortune that generated random numbers. A big number was selected, and estimates went up. They discovered that with the wheel, they could influence their subjects' responses.[9] Other samples can be, a condom with signage of *95%*

effective is more marketable than the one with a label of *5% chance of failure*. Or it sounds more frightening when there is a *70% chance of an earthquake* rather than *30% of not having one* — the bigger the figure, the more likely that it affects our perspective.

Framing can affect the way we see things and how we handle them. The famous golf player Tiger Woods once said that if you don't feel nervous, that means you don't care. Patients that undergo psychotherapy are often instructed to frame a situation that can be a challenge or an opportunity. The research found that patients who do such simulations are stronger in the face of stress. Words are good examples of frames because they create various mental schemas. Like euphemisms which are effective frames because their purpose is to distract and to lessen the weight of something offensive or unpleasant. An example is a good veterinarian, instead of saying that he "killed" your pet because of the complications of cancer, he would likely to say, "I put your pet to sleep."

Aside from the words, the overall tone of the language is a powerful frame in association with the different origins that built the term. For instance, the general and scientific Post Traumatic Stress Disorder that was used during the Vietnam War originated from Shell Shock and Battle Fatigue during World Wars I and II respectively. Framing is an inevitable process because we always have a point of view in everything that we know, and it forms biases the way we see things around us. Of course, once biases are structured, we omit or devalue other situations or ideas. Always keep in mind that we have the power to win against the unexpected pitfalls of framing. That is why you have to be careful because if you don't keep an eye on the framing battle, you will become the biggest loser. First thing first, you have to be aware that the framing saga is always around and present all the time. Awareness of what is happening in your environment makes you prepared and gives the control back to you. It is also possible that you make it a habit to study and to collect different frames that you can use to understand a situation and your future decisions.

For Your Application...

I interviewed a friend of mine and her name is Lalaine. She is currently working as vice-president of a pre-press company located in Maryland, USA. She gladly recounted to me the lesson she learned from being an impulsive leader.

Lalaine is a Vice-President for more than a decade now. A single mother of two, she has a maternal instinct for her subordinates, but she is also strict during working hours. In her earlier years as a VP, she checked her employees and their production by roaming around the company premises and silently observing the employees. It is a normal scenario for her to see employees, who are not aware of her presence, eating in their workstation and that is a violation of company rule; employees who are talking about things that are not work-related; and the worst, those who are sleeping and those who are having *extracurricular activities* during production time. So, she used to raise these issues to her supervisors and they gladly complied. Then, after a week or less, the employees were coming back on their unprofessional habits. After a few years, *CCTV cameras* became a trendy monitoring system and Lalaine was happy to see the company attached CCTV cameras in every corner of the company. Since the installation of the cameras, Lalaine decided not to roam discreetly within the company premises and stay longer at her station to work. Lalaine was very vigilant and she took advantage of the CCTVs. She watched her employees from her computer monitor and she often called the attention of those people who are violating company rules and remind them to focus back to work.

There was this one department that was causing a lot of headaches to Lalaine. On her computer monitor, she noticed that a lot from this department was not focusing on their assigned projects and it seemed that they were constantly moving from one station to another. She got a suspicion that they were just talking things that were not work-related. Since production time was recorded to an online system, she asked their IT personnel to generate a productivity report of the employees involved to see how productive they were. According to the data, some of them were productive, some had suspicious records. Before the report came into her hands, she already had a confirmation bias and the things she witnessed in the video recordings allowed her to frame that some of her employees were not working seriously. No matter how good their productivity time, they can do much better if they will just focus on their tasks. She also got reports about noise issues from other departments. She raised this issue to the supervisor in-charge to investigate and take necessary measures in case the employees were not focusing and if the reports were true.

The supervisor held a meeting with the employees involved and informed them about Lalaine's observations and the concerns of other departments. According to them, they needed to switch places in some instances because the applications that they were running were compatible with other computers that were vital for their tasks. They also cleared the issue that was noisy and rebutted that they have to discuss work-related matters as a group and they didn't think that whispering out was enough just to please other departments. They also became honest that they were having a friendly chat to kill boredom, to refresh their brains, and to avoid themselves from sleeping because the atmosphere sometimes was inviting them to take a nap. Moreover, they didn't have any backlogs so far and they finished their projects on or ahead of time.

The supervisor discussed this to Lalaine during a meeting with the HR supervisor. After Lalaine heard the side of the employees involved, she understood now the situation. She decided that in order to avoid moving stations, a seating plan must be applied for the convenience of her employees and to maximize their production. Regarding the noise issue, the HR supervisor defended the employees because she overheard once the extent of the discussion that they were having, and it was work-related. She also realized that having a little friendly talk is okay as long as the production is not compromised, and due dates are assured to meet on time. Anyway, that was the productivity report suggested so far. Lalaine soon became more open-minded and instead of constantly relying on the CCTV footage, she went back to silently roam to conduct a surprise inspection, a routine she hadn't done for so many years.

Instead of being clouded with assumptions and false judgments, it is best in a corporate setting to see things in actual and to rely on a practical basis. Before jumping on into conclusions, it is best to investigate if there are suspicious actions to prevent hurting the feelings of the people around you who are doing their best. Providing a friendly work environment to employees will set a good production rate and quality output as long as company rules are enforced correctly.

Chapter 3 – Answering All These Questions

To lead yourself to the ladder of progression is not easy and you need to face painstaking battles along your path to gain approval or promotion from most of the people you are working with. In the corporate world or any work environment, there is a famous saying that I know you are already familiar with which is essential for aspiring leaders. There was once a wise man who said, "***A good leader is a good follower***." In my experience, listening to instructions and taking down reminders are vital in successfully completing a specific task. To be a good leader as well, you must be strong no matter what failure comes in and it is important to learn from mistakes. Leadership means that you are responsible for anything that is related to you. If it is hard to lead yourself, it is much harder to lead people or to lead a territory and to secure them.

Doing things for the very first time reciprocates more room for errors and knowledge to accommodate. Let me give you a list of the common mistakes of beginning leaders that you might be doing, or you will probably encounter once you have a promotion. So, grab your highlighter and mark those that interest you.[1]

1. ***Always make yourself presentable.*** It is a common mistake for beginning leaders to be intimidated by their officemates because of the new position that has been given to them. No matter how good your outfit is, if you are not wearing self-confidence, you put yourself in deeper scrutiny making you uncomfortable as a result. So, communicate with eye contact, make an appropriate facial expression, and speak with confidence. How you present yourself and deal with others speak a lot about you.

2. ***Maximize your time learning from your mentors.*** Most of the time, we get intimidated by the leaders who train us. Training is important, especially when you are about to handle more complicated and demanding tasks. Typically, during promotion, you need to fill in someone's position which is either promoted or resigned. Instead of being a keen listener and observer, be inquisitive and always ask questions if there is something that is not clear enough or you do not understand completely. Review your manual and modules ahead of time so that, you can validate things that are not thoroughly discussed. It is best as well if you will ask for advice and techniques for you to become more effective.

3. ***Don't let your failures put you down.*** Failure is important for you to learn more and grow as a person, always keep that in mind. Nobody is perfect and even the biggest CEOs' and leaders around

the globe are imperfect who committed perfect mistakes. Your mistakes also allow you to be more compassionate with your subordinates who are aspiring to be leaders as well.

4. ***Do not be complacent.*** Once you officially take over a position and you learned the things that you must learn, it is time for you to put yourself to the test. If you are handling a safe or prosperous team or territory, do not be contented with what your predecessors achieved and established. You must think of other ways that will make you unforgettable in a positive manner. Do not be stagnant like most of the leaders around you. You must act and make a difference!

5. ***Take time to pause and to think.*** Overall management is part of leadership and that makes it tedious, demanding, and somewhat exhausting. Whenever you feel drain and tired because of how busy you are, find some time to breathe out.

Relaxation helps you to think correctly and that equates in making wise and correct decisions. Resetting your whole system will make you fully prepared again for tackling any challenges.

6. ***Do not be so judgmental and impulsive, be transparent.*** Remember Lalaine in my previous example? When you hear reports about your subordinate(s), conduct your own investigation and ask the persons or parties involved. Do not be judgmental and make assumptions, especially when your favorite one spilled the beans. Assumptions often lead to more and complicated conflicts. So, be transparent and be an ambassador of peace.

7. ***Don't let your position get into your head.*** If you are a fan of *Game of Thrones*, you are familiar with the *mother of dragons*, Daenerys Targaryen. Her lady-in-waiting and confidant used to enumerate her titles to tell how important and entitled

she was. As the series goes, her emotional breakdown and too much entitlement led to her demise. As a leader, you become humble at first. Stay that way no matter how long you are in that position. Always remember that respect is earned and not imposed.

8. ***Be careful in accepting advice.*** As everybody does, we get advice from people who are really close to us. In the corporate environment, listening to people who don't know the extent of an issue leads to managerial downfall. To get wise advice, you must ask yourself if the person is connected, competent, and candid.

9. ***Believe in yourself.*** Be bold and take the risk to your sure ideas. Instead of being discovered, you must act and discover your own success.

10. ***Explore.*** Do not just be stagnant and explore other areas of your field or the areas of other fields. Life is a learning process, and so is leadership. The more you

learned, the more you will become effective. Staying in the same territory brings boredom and dissatisfaction.

Some of the problems I enumerated above are inevitable and vital for your growth. Just make sure that it won't happen again unless you are trapped in a very difficult situation. The question is, what are you going to do to prevent yourself from repeating the same mistakes? Well, it's time for me to give you the mental models that have been effective and still used by successful people in different industries.

Mental Model #1: The First Principles

One of the best ways of thinking that have been effectively used by Charlie Munger and Elon Musk is the *first principles*. This mental model was used as early as the ancient times and was famously used by the famous philosophers in history like Aristotle. Its function is to reverse-engineer complex situations and establishes creative opportunities. Also known as *reasoning from first principles*, it dissects complex problems into basic parts and assembles them back once the root of the element has been revealed. This method allows you to think for your own, unleash your creativity, and provides non-linear outcomes.

A first principle is a root assumption or information that can also stand alone. It cannot also be deduced from another assumption. Perception by first principles omits the unnecessary elements of propositions. Through this, what is surely left is of importance. It is one of the most effective mental models that you can utilize to improve your perception and the way you see things in a deeper manner. First-principles can be explained further using **the coach and the player scenario**.

A game coach creates the game itself because it is the one who thinks what to do best in order to win against the opposing team. A coach assesses the physical possibilities, the strength, and weaknesses of the opponent, and create a strategy that is formulated to give a team an advantage. Creating strategies is a risk and each of them must be tested in order to find what works for a certain situation. Every coach has its basis from the first principles. Every game has its rules and these rules are the first principles. Rules dictate what you can and cannot do in a game. You can do everything as long as it is legal and conforms with the rules. Players are to execute the tactic presented by the coach. The coach and the player are separate entities and they generate different results. The coach can analyze why a game is successful or not and is capable of adjusting his tactics while the player doesn't generally have an idea about what is going on and what is working or not since he completely relies on the coach. We are in the segment between coach and player who reason by first principles, by analogy, or a combination of both. The first principle of reasoning breaks through tradition and brings light to the darkness. While reasoning from analogy is so traditional and it might lead you further from the answer that you are seeking for. Utilizing it will help you see the world from a deeper perspective and be more open-minded to possibilities. We are rational beings and some of us hesitate to take advice from the people around us. It is because their experiences are different from our own and we see things differently.

There are various techniques to establish first principles effectively. On top is **Socratic questioning** using stringent analysis. A disciplined questioning process, it is used to establish truths, reveal hidden assumptions, and divide knowledge from unfamiliarity. Socratic questioning pursues to detect first principles is an organized manner. You can also use the **Five**

Whys which is very common to children whose inquisition is unstoppable unless satisfied.

Since we always want social validation, the bits of advice and thoughts of others suppress us if we don't know how to be independent and think for our own. Reasoning using first principles enables you to get out of the past and traditional wisdom. You could have the tendency to see what is possible when you understand the underlying principles and utilize your own methods or mental models. Reasoning by first principles is best when you are trying something as your very first; facing difficulties, and trying to understand things that you are not used to. You can eradicate those problems if you stop making guesses and prevent others from getting into your head. With the first principles, it unleashes the creative part of you and sets you free from analogies which is a good start for you to understand more deeply. You are also more likely to come up with better answers, adapt to changes, accept reality, and bolder to grab opportunities.

Elon Musk and His First Principles2

Elon Reeve Musk was born on June 28, 1971, in South Africa. He is currently residing in Los Angeles, California and a father of six. He is known to be one of the boldest entrepreneurs this world has ever witnessed. Being a founder and heading some of the most successful companies like SpaceX, he seems unstoppable. Musk was recognized by Forbes as one of the most powerful and richest people in the world. With a jaw-dropping net worth of $19 billion, everybody wants to know his secret.

He believes that in order to understand reality, you should start with what is true. He begins with what he wants to achieve and traces the first principles of the problem. A true visionary, Musk wanted to send people to Mars, and he found rockets absurdly expensive. He wanted to make cheaper ones. So, he studied what rockets are made of and only to find out that they two percent higher of the original price. There was no stopping Musk to create cheaper rockets. He is a studious person and has a degree in economics and physics, and he taught himself rocket science. That led him to establish SpaceX to see if he could build cheaper rockets.

Musk utilized the first principles in SpaceX to have gradual changes at low costs. According to his blueprint, battery packs are expensive, and they will always be because that's the way it has been which is pretty dumb. Because when you applied it to new things like a car, you cannot just say that horses are great, and it is a way better than cars because we're used to it. That's very traditional reasoning. So, in order for him to save more and to fulfill his visions, he gave an interesting example with battery packs. Traditionally, they are worth $600 per kilowatt-hour. To understand its price, he used first principles by breaking down the problem's components and their actual price in the market. So, the batteries got cobalt, aluminum, polymers, nickel, carbon, and steel can. These materials are available at the London Metal Exchange for an affordable price of $80 per kilowatt-hour. He said that you just need to be clever to acquire those materials and combine them to create a battery cell. There you have cheaper batteries.

In an interview with Larry Page, he was amazed at Musk because he is unusual and he also knowledgeable in business, organization, governmental, and leadership issues.

Mental Model #2: The Thought Experiment

Thought experiments, just like our first mental model which is the first principle, can be traced back as early as the dominance of ancient Greeks and Romans.[3] This mental model helped them to enrich some of humanity's greatest innovation and advances from philosophy to physics. A thought experiment is actually a way of exploring an idea, concept, or hypothesis by deep thought. When looking for practical evidence seems unattainable, the best way is to utilize thought experiments to understand complex ideas. Its purpose is to promote rational thinking, assumptions, and to alter models. Once used, it might also help you to come out of your comfort zone because it will allow you to realize that you must confront reality and to find answers to your questions that you have difficulty to answer. This mental model reveals to us that there are limitations on what we know and there are things that we cannot identify.

There are different types of thought experiments.

(1) *prefactual* which involves potential outcomes;

(2) *counterfactual* which is contradicting facts;

(3) *semi-factual* that contemplates if a different past can still lead to the present;

(4) *prediction* that theorizing future products based on available data;

(5) *hindcasting* that runs a reverse prediction to find out if it predicted a situation that had already happened;

(6) *retrodiction* that moves backward from a situation to find out the root cause; and lastly,

(7) *backcasting* that considers an outcome and works on the present to assume its causes.

Thought experiments are highly important in philosophy and integral to its evolution since ancient times. They provide answers to subjective philosophical hypotheses that empirical evidence cannot. Philosophers utilize this mental model to convey philosophies easy to understand. The goal of thought experiments is to illustrate a particular concept, like free will, and dive into abstracted situations. The goal is to create new ideas and not to dismantle what is proven to be correct. Plato provided an early example of a philosophical thought experiment known as the *Allegory of the Cave*. The narrative goes with a group of people who were born and live within the confines of a dark cave. Living in that cave for most of their existence, they saw nothing but shadows. They don't have any idea what's outside and they don't want to leave the cave either. A time comes that they were led outside, only to realize that the world is more than mere shadows and that the world is far more intriguing and so has much to offer. If these cavemen returned to the cave, their lives would be very different and unsatisfactory. They will start to regret that they went out. Plato used this allegory to convey his great appreciation of educating ourselves. That our first move to get out of the dark cave is dismantling ourselves to be educated and start to seek things that would help us understand the world.

Thought experiments have been helpful as well in the field of science. Empirical pieces of evidence are vital for this body of knowledge while experiments are used to create hypotheses. There are hypotheses that cannot be tested like the string theory. This mental model is often used by theoretical scientists to provide a provisional answer. Andrew D. Irvine is a Canadian academic who wrote a paper entitled *Thought Experiments in Scientific Reasoning*. He explained that this mental model is a key part of science which is in the same territory as physical experiments. It wants all assumptions to be reinforced by empirical evidence. The idea must be feasible and must give answers to intricate questions. A thought experiment must have the capacity to be wrong. An example of a thought experiment is *Schrodinger's Cat* that was developed in 1935 by Edwin Schrodinger. This experiment wants to show the counterintuitive part of quantum mechanics in a more accessible manner. The experiment goes with a cat, which can be alive or dead, inserted within a box. In the box, you will see a small amount of decaying radioactive material and a Geiger counter. Over time, the radioactive material may decay or not. If it decays, a tube of acid will crash and poison the animal. Without even opening the box, it is impossible to find out if the cat is dead or alive. The only indication that we have is the angry cat will start meowing if it is alive. Like the majority of experiments, details are subjective. Schrodinger's wanted to imply that quantum mechanics are unclassified. According to the astrophysicist John Gribbin, nothing is real unless it is scrutinized and that there is no underlying reality in the word. Schrodinger himself also stated that we do not fit into this material world that science created for all of us because we are outside of it. We are just its audience who can be amazed, shocked, or scared to its revelations. We believed that we are all part of it because we see ourselves in the picture.

Albert Einstein and His Application of Thought Experiments

Albert Einstein was a theoretical physicist and is considered as one, if not the most, famous physicist of all time. He is forever associated with the scientific world because he provided the modern foundation of physics: the theory of relativity.

Einstein was born on March 14, 1879, in Germany. Since childhood, Einstein was an exceptional student who greatly had an interest in math and physics. He then took math and physics in college at Federal Polytechnic School and a Ph.D. at the University of Zurich. The year 1905 was the turning point of Einstein's career as a physicist. He published the Annus Mirabilis papers which contained four articles that contributed greatly to the foundation of modern physics. These articles are Photoelectric Effect, Mass-Energy Equivalence, Brownian Motion and the Special Theory of Relativity. It also included the famous equation, $E=mc^2$.

The thought experiments mental model helped Einstein to his important discoveries. The most famous where he applied the thought experiments were on a beam of light that was later made into a brilliant kids' book. He asked himself, "What would happen if you catch a beam of light as it moved?" As he was looking for the answer, it led him to a different course that changed his life forever and benefited the field of physics as well. And the special theory of relativity was born. His services for the advancement of physics made him a Nobel laureate.

Mental Model #3: The Second-Order Thinking

As humans, it is our common trait to be judgmental and we often believe in what we initially see. As the saying goes with *what you see is what you get*. But we must keep in mind that there is something more beneath the surface and that things aren't always as they seem. There were times that we tried to solve a problem and we end up accidentally making room for another one that is even worse. The best method to check the long-term effects of our options is to utilize **second-order thinking**.

It is easier to recognize when you didn't consider right away the second and consequent order influences. For example, in business, there is a narcissistic boss who always wanted attention, but he doesn't want to work that much and be more active in his other activities. To secure that his presence is still active in the company, he created a right-hand that will manage and oversee on his behalf. Being the right-hand means that you are powerful enough to do your boss's function. The right hand is always present in the company and always attends to the needs of the employees that he gained the respect and loyalty of them. One day, the boss stayed at the office and observed how warmth the employees' greetings to his right hand compared to him. He realized that the affection of the people that he always wanted went to his right hand. It was not a good move after all for someone who is always craving attention.

The capacity to analyze things in the midst of challenges to the second, third, fifth, until infinity and beyond, is a powerful device that charges and expand your thinking. If there is second thinking, it is a good thing if you are asking yourself about the first one. First-level thinking is very simple and shallow; every one of us can apply it. First-level thinkers are already satisfied with the opinions of the people around them.

Second-order thinking demands a lot of action because it is difficult to think in terms of time, principles, and connections. Applying this mental model means that you are intelligent to divide yourself from the rest. It helps you to improve your ability to think by constantly asking yourself and by thinking through time.

Ray Dalio and His Application of the Second-Order Thinking

Raymond Dalio was born on August 8, 1949, in New York City. A son of a musician, he started investing as early as the age of 12 when he decided to buy some shares of Northeast Airlines for $300. This investment went tripled when the airlines tied with another company. He later received his bachelor's degree in finance from Long Island University and his MBA from

Business School. Today, Dalio is a billionaire investor who founded the world's largest hedge-fund firm, Bridgewater Associates.

The second-order thinking philosophy helped Dalio to reach the peak of his success by choosing what he wanted in life and avoid temptations no matter how hard to ignore them. Like, if you want to be healthy and more attractive, you must avoid eating too much and conduct a proper diet as well as regular exercise so you can achieve the appearance that you want. This is how Dalio became a mogul in the business world. He always thinks first the implications of his decisions before he put them into action.

Mental Model #4: The Probabilistic Thinking

We are living in a world where countless unexpected events are being ruled by a dynamic set of influences. We need a mental model that would help us predict what would happen the most likely, and **probabilistic thinking** is a perfect fit for the job. If you are mathematically and philosophically inclined, I could say that this is the best mental model for you. Probabilistic thinking is vitally attempting to estimate, with the help of math and logic, the incoming situation. It is one of the mental models that improve the accuracy and success of our decisions.

We are short of perfect information about the world and this fact makes way to all the existing probability theory. We don't have the power to see the future as accurately as psychics do. The best possible way that we can do is to estimate what lies ahead with the help of practical and realistic probabilities.[6]

Thomas Bayes and Bayesian Thinking

Thomas Bayes was born in 1702 in London, United Kingdom. His alma mater is the University of Edinburgh. He was a notable English minister in the early half of the 18th century and he was famous for publishing An Essay Toward Solving a Problem in the Doctrine of Chances. In 1973, two years after his death, a friend named Richard Price, a British philosopher, was very impressed and brought the paper to the attention of the Royal Society. The essay paved the way to the Bayes Theorem which is concerned with how we will adjust probabilities when we come across new data.

The very core of Bayesian thinking lies with the thought that, by default, we have limited but convenient information about the world, and we are continuously meeting new ideas. We keep on believing that before the new idea pops out, we are already knowledgeable. This mental model enables us to utilize what is essential material in making decisions.

Mental Model #5: The Inversion Principle

The ***Inversion Principle*** is based on a proverb *"invert, always invert"* by the German mathematician Carl Gustav Jacobi. This mental model has been highly promoted by Charlie Munger. According to him, in solving a problem, it is important to approach the issue from the opposite side. By this tactic, it will ensure that you have thought everything that would greatly hinder you from achieving your goal. What we conventionally do is to confront problems starting from where it begins. It is highly suggested that we could make a different approach and start backward. By inversion, you have to think of the worst possible problems in order to provide probable effective solutions.

There are three easy steps for you to apply the inversion principle to develop better output. You should **define the problem** first. Then **invert it** thinking the worst possible problem you could encounter. Lastly, **consider the solutions** that you can apply during the second step.

The Evolution of the Inversion Principle

It was in 63-65 AD when Stoic philosophers practiced the *premeditation Malorum* or premeditation of evils to oversee the worst factors that could affect every event. Then here comes the fast forward, it was in 1820 when the German mathematician Carl Jacobi stated that complex problems could be verified by inverting them. The famous Charlie Munger has made Jacobi's maxim widely known over the past twenty years. In 1989, Deborah Mitchell, Jay Russo, and Nancy Pennington discovered that event imagination boosts the capacity to recognize reasons for possible results. While Gary Klein, a psychologist, and best-selling author, in 2004 proposed a pre-mortem guide to prospective hindsight. Tim Ferris in 2017 provided premeditation malorum an easier name and guide in his TED talk. He believes in the sequence identify fears, benefits of risks, and loss of inaction.

Mental Model #6: The Loss Aversion/Fairness/Endowment Effect

We all hate to lose things, especially those that are very important to us. Repeated sequence of losing is even more painful while gaining gives us pleasure. When you acquire something, it becomes a member of your system and ***loss aversion/fairness/endowment effect*** is responsible for that process. As these materials become part of you, you value it more than the way if they were not yours. You become angry seeing them taken away from you more than you would appreciate them being given to you. Individuals have a powerful inherent sense of fairness which is connected to their right they believe they have control over. Whenever you break this sense of fairness, it can lead to the development of *deprival super-reaction syndrome*. This syndrome is always associated with the loss of fairness and you tend to shout the words, "*It's unfair!*"

This mental model allows you to be more helpful to others while helping yourself at the same time. You know the feeling of being in pain of losing and you become more empathic with others. By understanding loss aversion, you find ways to help people overcome their agony or you can think of solutions to help them without giving up anything. With this, successful negotiation outcomes may come on the way.

In the corporate industry, you may apply it to win some deals by preparing proposals that lead to a win-win situation.

Understanding About Deprival Super-reaction Syndrome

Charles Schulz, creator of the comic strip "Peanuts", created a panel where his famous Peanut character, Lucy, was deprived of her birthday party and she said, "it's not fair!" then she had tantrums instead of understanding her mother, a very typical reaction of a child who didn't get what she badly wants. This is a classic example of deprival super-reaction syndrome which is always partnered by exclamations of unfairness which paves the way for us to believe that individuals have a sense of fairness.

According to Richard Thaler, an American economist, economists believed that fairness was a senseless concept mostly utilized by children who don't get what they wanted. Going back to Lucy, for her, it is not fair that her mother didn't keep her promise that Lucy will be having a birthday party. There is really an essential angle on expectations with our sample. It is crystal clear that Lucy held on to her mother's promise and that she had a right to have a birthday party. That is actually a part of her endowment –– or her rights and possessions.

When you have something and you have the natural or legal rights to own it and suddenly taken away from you, it is normal for you to feel unfairness. Going back to the Peanuts comic strip, when can see the fact that Lucy will celebrate her birthday once a year like everyone does, therefore, she didn't always have to do it that it became a good reason for her to expect. The mere fact that the comic strip specified that the party was promised, it became a part of her endowment since it was promised. So, hypothetically, what Lucy might have felt and done are quite rebellious to show that the promise was violated. She was definitely not happy, didn't even talk to her mom, felt betrayed and left behind, shamed on herself because her friends were expecting the party, didn't do her daily chores back at home, and a lot more than you can imagine. It is clear that the anguish and agony experienced by Lucy upon the cancellation of her birthday party greatly exceeded the pleasure she once felt when the party was announced and promised by her mom.

Mental Model #7: The Sunk Costs/Commitment + Consistency Bias

The concept of this mental model can be easily explained. Time and money are vital to our existence and you cannot take them back once you spend them or they're **sunk costs.** Since you cannot take them back, you have to focus and spend your energy on other things like building for your future. Sunk costs, if not fully understood and utilized correctly, can lead you down to horrible situations like despair, and death as the worst implication. The best example that history can offer us is the wars that destroyed many lives, including our natural resources. War is very expensive and destructive. Teaching yourselves to have a practical intuition of sunk costs aids you to think of better decisions. Sunk costs as a mental model is a kind of trait that you can utilize in certain situations like other models.

Consistency bias which is also called as *thesis drift* goes with the concept that you are doing an action for a better cause, but this reason changes eventually, and you are still doing the same thing. It usually garbles your decision-making. In a different course, you can utilize that situation to advertise unity, but you should be aware that the implications of small actions can make way to sunk costs that you have to justify.

Richard Feynman and His Sunk Costs

Richard Phillips Feynman was born on May 11, 1918, in New York. He was a theoretical physicist and his contributions in the field of physics led him to earn the Nobel Prize for Physics in 1965.

Feynman assisted the US in developing the atomic bomb known as the *Manhattan Project.* He experienced sunk costs in this project. He joined the project because he saw the Germans as dangers in society. He felt immoral because along with the success of the project and the defeat of Germany, he forgot the reason why he supported the project. Since the successful launched of the atomic bomb in Hiroshima and Nagasaki, they partied and got drunk while so many innocent people were dying in Japan.

Mental Model #8: Product vs. Packaging/Action Bias

If you are a shopaholic and you bought something, you used to ignore and throw away the packaging without reading it to enjoy the product within it. Practically, others scrutinize the packaging that tells the totality of the product. This mental model gives you another way of getting ideas which is adaptive. But you must also be aware that in some instances, it can lead you to odd and irrational behavior. For example, being industrious without being productive or counterproductive. If probabilistic thinking suggests that we must begin making analysis by focusing on the packaging, the ***product vs. packaging*** mental model recommends that we need to take our analysis to a different level to ensure that the product is what the packaging says.

Product vs. packaging enables you to have some time thinking about situations intellectually and emotionally. For example in a corporate setting, overproduction is not good because it leads to major problems with throughput, inventory, and other various aspects. Sometimes the more you act, the more your situation becomes complicated. That doing more is worse than doing nothing at all. This mental model is highly related to one of the paradigms formulated by Stephen Covey and that is, *to begin with the end in mind.* You must know your destination, where your decisions will lead you. Always be observant because you might be working very hard to reach the far end of the ladder to progression, only to find out that it is leading you in the wrong direction.

So, whether you are a leader or a member of a team, your focus should always be on **how to be more effective** and **not on how to be busy**. Culturally, we tend to connect busyness to being more productive, even though in reality that it is stressful and generally bad. Bad because being busy doesn't always lead you in the right direction. Sometimes, giving heavy labor to your workload, you tend to forget the most important things that you must accomplish or even the essence of why you are working.

Stephen Covey and His Stand on Busyness vs. Productivity

Stephen Covey is a motivational author who became famous for his best-selling book entitled The 7 Habits of Highly Effective People. This book has relations with different mental models including a deeper understanding of product vs. packaging in the specific area of busyness vs. productivity. Almost an entire chapter was dedicated to it.

Covey provided a four-quadrant model in his book and we will focus on three of the specific elements.

- **Butt in chair** – proposes that some deeds are more valuable than others. This element agrees that most of our best accomplishments are a product of creativity and novelty. Doing too much work and we have no time to think creatively and acquire a far greater perspective about our surroundings.
- **Visible Markers** – It is a cliché that in order to prove that we are making progress, we have to do and acquire a lot of things. This element conforms with that idea, as long as we see our progress in visible markers. This element is observed when we accomplish things that give us satisfaction and motivation to do more because of a sense of purpose.
- **Type of day** – This element greatly depends on the discussion of chronotypes — a term that actually used in zoology that refers to the time when animals are active or inactive.10

In the corporate world, it determines if you are an early bird or a night owl. This element discusses when we are more productive and creative. Our body clock is our label for the productivity that we can offer in an organization.

Mental Model #9: The Base Rates

A ***Base Rate*** mental model is a form of probability that defines the possibility of an event when new or more accurate information is lacking. This mental model covers the highly likely chance that something might or might not happen, which doesn't conform with the recent information that might change the possibility that essential for an expected event. Therefore, base rates tell what commonly happens if nothing is available to influence the outcome. Part of this mental model is **the base rate**

fallacy which refers to our capacity to ignore information that allows us to predict what could happen because we tend to concentrate on the latest, previous, and fascinating data instead. ***Bayes Theorem*** also comes helpful in this mental model since it is a mathematical equation wherein you can include the Base Rate for a situation with the possibilities associated with the latest data to extract the actual total possibility for a predicted event.[10] One example that we can have is the probability of the gross income of an established company.

Utilizing this mental model will help you to become more ready and equipped with solutions that you might encounter in case that your Base Rates predicted a not-so-good outcome for your future endeavors. Being highly prepared will give you prestige among your workmates because of your strategic analysis of things that are still on the way.

For Your Application...

Now that you have learned about other mental models that have been utilized by different business tycoons and other prominent luminaries in different fields, you can enhance your ability to lead and to have a more positive perspective in any situation that you will be involved as you live each day.

The First Principles mental model allows you to trace the very roots of a situation for better understanding and for you to find a more creative decision. And to be creative, you have learned under the **Product vs. Packaging** a deeper knowledge about **Busyness vs. Productivity** that you must have time to relax to be more creative and not to be eaten by working too hard without even knowing the very purpose of your labor. In a corporate setting, your problems are not answerable by just one answer or a single mental model. To find a solution that would fit your problem, the

Thought Experiment teaches you to explore ideas, concepts, and hypotheses, then apply them to various situations, and identify what really works on which. Upon the identification of effective mental models, the **Second-Order Thinking** leads you not to be contented with what you see on the surface, but to dig more and see the lifelong impact of your decisions. The **Probabilistic Thinking** and **Base Rates** show you the imminent use of previous data to form new information by forensic prediction of future outcomes. Solving issues from the start can sometimes lead you to a more difficult situation. You can utilize the **Inversion Principle** and change your perspective by dealing backward to form a decision. The **Loss Aversion/Fairness/Endowment Effect** and **Sunk Costs/Commitment + Consistency Bias** mental models make you a good leader by putting yourself first in the position of others that allows you to be empathic. Through this, you gain more information about the situation enabling you to create win-win decisions and proposals. And those are the powers you have to unlock and learn more from these mental models.

Chapter 4 – Optimizing and Systemizing Productivity

Leaders are given the hardest tasks that demand the most complex decisions. That is why they tend to do everything on their own and without relying absolutely on their subordinates. This is a common habit of beginning leaders. They want to do every bit of the job and make it perfect all at once to prove that they deserve their promotion. They want to win the respect of all and secure the good projection of their image before they rest and create other leaders. Because of such impulse, they are also prone to errors and put themselves in difficult situations. Most of the time, they exude too much confidence and self-glorification that they make decisions directly, without thinking a million times and without asking for help from their superiors. They work too much, and they think a lot that they even bring their jobs at home and constantly think about work. They cannot sleep properly at all and they sometimes lock themselves away from their social circle. Committing such suicide leads to possible burnouts.

I don't want you to mess up your life while assuming your professional duties. That's why I prepared more mental models and healthy suggestions that will allow you to enjoy your corporate and personal lives. First, let's begin with **stress**.

1. Dealing with Stress

You may always associate stress with your career, your boss, the deadlines that you have to meet, and other personal factors that are demanding your full attention. These factors are constantly giving you so many headaches and confusion to the point that you want to divide your body to accommodate them all. The stress that you identify, brought by trying your best to meet important matters, shouldn't be considered stress at all. What you are feeling is **pressure**. Pressure, as defined by Merriam-Webster, *is the burden of physical or mental distress.*[1] There is no inherent stress even if the demand could be intense. You can avoid stress or let go of it easily if you know how to react to pressure and the sudden changes in life. You always have options to choose from. Always remember that you have to be resilient or flexible and the key to it is to avoid converting pressure into stress. The number one cause of stress is **rumination**.

Rumination

Mental process of repeated thinking about something negatively. The basic symptom of rumination includes waking up in the middle night and having difficulty going back to sleep because of the things you haven't and should have done. I know that you have experienced this because I myself had been in the same situation many times! Rumination can also bring back the past that contains negativity and worries that don't do any good. Individuals who don't ruminate could be suffering from a lot of difficulties by they are not stressed by it. For you to prevent rumination and to live a better life and lead effectively, I prepared a list of mental habits to reduce your stress and intensify your resilience.[2]

1. ***Live in the present.*** You have to wake up and live in the present, live in reality. Do not let your past hinder your present that will affect your future. Admit it or not, we have dull moments that we daydream. We look back at things and regret some of our decisions in the past and we conjure that ***what if? question***. It gives us stress most of the time because we feel bad for things that help us grow somehow. Gather yourself and focus back on your present and be positive about your future. Living in the

present will help you to see the real mechanism of the world.

2. ***Be always in control.*** Once you gather yourself and come back in the present, do not be distracted to things that won't contribute to your growth, to your production, and that will take too much of your time that cause you no good. It is correct that we are not in control of what will happen to us, but you have the power to control your attention. So, practice attentively on putting your attention to the most important things and strategize for your long-term happiness and success. Being in control will also help you to predict and manipulate the odds when you make decisions.

3. ***Believe in the power of distance.*** If you the irrational and distressed about someone or something, then you have to save yourself and create a space and distance yourself from things that keep

you away from the peace you deserve. Detachment gives you the ability to preserve yourself and to maintain your perspective. Sometimes, we are not aware that we are investing a great deal of our time and energy into things and people that are temporary. They the things are keeping us from growing because that's the way we like it. If these things are causing you stress and you feel tired and toxic because of their out-of-place demands, it is time for you to detach. As long as you keep things that are unhealthy for you physically, mentally, emotionally, and spiritually, you are prone to commit errors that will also affect your relationship to others and your performance at work. Do not allow your emotions and your past to hinder your journey towards growth. So, detach and gain yourself once more to reflect and strategize than to ruminate.

4. **Breakaway.** There are mental models that we are using in order to solve our problems professionally or mentally. If you find some methods that are ineffective and causing you more trouble like being pessimistic, learn to break away and let go of things that give you more suffering. Aside from what your brain is projecting, let go as well from uncertainties, negative emotions, and bad habits that do not contribute to your growth and might also affect your capability to decide efficiently.

5. **Be occupied with positivity.** Another thing that you must practice is to be occupied. Being occupied in a way that won't burn you out but will help you propagate success. So, in case you are facing a problem, then play along with time and think of strategies that will help you out from that situation. Conduct a SWOT (Strengths, Weaknesses, Opportunities, and Threats) analysis for

you to identify every angle of your decision. If you are in a very harmonious situation, then think of things that will sustain the happiness that you are enjoying. Positivity reflects not only for you and with everyone around you.

6. ***Always be adrift.*** Remember that problems are always just around the corner and they can offer you growth and lessons that you will value for the rest of your life. If you are being flooded by overthinking or rumination, do not get drowned no matter how strong the current is. Open your mind, have high hopes, and be optimistic –– these things will help you get above them all. Self-preservation and your goals in life allow you to find the best strategies to attain what you want in life.

- ***Reflect.*** The mind is a very powerful organ and whatever we feed to it, dictates the outcome. If we think negatively, we feel doubt and uncertainties that lead us to problems and regrets. When we think positively, we become much stronger and empowered resulting in success and good decisions. Ruminating does you no good and it will constantly give you setbacks and uncertainties. Reflection serves you with a purpose by getting ahead and a plan for a brighter future, and acknowledge that your shortcomings are your springboard in achieving your goals. Reflection is also a healthy way to activate your senses and make them in harmony with your mind. It causes relaxation and you can find better solutions to problems that you find exhausting.

2. Be Highly Concerned About Mental Health

Thinking too much about work, aside from your personal matters, brings many possible mental issues. Overdoing tasks, working beyond your capacity, bullying, and paranoia are some of the possible factors that can affect your mental health. Leaders are models and should set as an example for everyone in the workplace. They are also responsible for promoting emotional and mental welfare. So, voicing these issues out in the workplace must be tolerated for the awareness of everyone and to help those who are in need. This is necessary to spread hope and empowerment. Aside from that, being a paragon of the importance of mental health awareness brings challenges for the promotion of such endeavors. You have to be highly prepared and informed about the facts concerning mental health so you can spot people who cannot directly announce that they are suffering from certain mental issues.

Below is the list that will help you to raise awareness and promote the importance of a healthy mental state.[3]

1. ***Show that you genuinely care.*** As a leader, you need to spend an ample

amount of time with your subordinates and bond with them. You can set a group dinner or team building to have quality time with them. You can ask and talk anything under the sun as long as you maintain everything professionally. Of course, you must be extra emotional and sentimental so they could feel your sincerity and show them that you actually care. I personally do a one-on-one talk to my trainees and often ask them about their professional insights and a bit about their personal lives. I found it very effective in establishing a strong rapport and letting them feel that as a leader, I am accessible and can respond to their professional needs. Providing your subordinates and coworkers with genuine care brings a more harmonious work environment and creativity. At the same time, you are building their confidence to trust and to look up to other professionals.

2. ***Be an open book and also share your struggles.*** It is a stigma that having mental issues equates to insanity. There are many leaders in history who struggled, and the difficulties they experienced helped them to be renowned pillars in their fields. According to the research conducted by a psychiatrist, Professor Nassir Ghaemi, people who are suffering from mental illness can be great leaders and can lead better. Mania unleashes creativity and resilience to trauma. Depression, on the other hand, intensifies empathy and practicality. To break such stigma, leaders must come forward and be an inspiration by sharing what they've been through to reach happiness and success. To act as a model reinforces people around you and to let them

know that there are others who are suffering as well and might be in greater difficulties. Sharing your struggles and how you succeed will give them the message that *there is a rainbow always after the rain.*

3. ***Be an advocate of self-love.*** Leaders must always be presentable and must command respect. Showing that you are always prepared because of good time management allows you to juggle with your professional and personal life efficiently. You can relax, have fun, have eight hours of sleep, and maintain an impressive physical, mental, emotional, and spiritual state. With these qualities, you are a model that everyone can follow for a healthier living. Also, showing warmth and compassion to your coworkers deepens your connection to them. Having very positive attributes can affect your surroundings and the people within

your circle that leads to a very good flow of business.

3. More Mental Models to Make Effective Decisions

It is time for me to unleash more mental models for you to create wise decisions that will resonate with a long-lasting impact not just to you, but everything around you. Effective and efficient decision-making processes are hard to find but once you recognize mental models and utilize them correctly, they will give you promising results. Unleash the great leader that has been dormant on your very core by reading the pointers ahead.

1. ***The Two-List System of Warren Buffet.*** Mr. Buffet had tried this with his pilot by asking him to create a list that contains his 25 most important things to accomplish and after doing

so, he was instructed to encircle his top 5 out of that 25. Later, this list was known as the two-list system. You have to segregate the more important priorities by having your **List A** and **List B** that contains the things you must avoid in order to accomplish the first list. Somehow, these lists are also reminders of the process of elimination. Reminders are great so you will be constantly reminded of the most important things that you must achieve and set aside those that are preventing you from attaining them.

2. ***The 10/10/10 Rule.*** You might have regrets about your past decisions because you didn't think about their long-term impact. This rule will help you to reflect on the long-term implications of your decisions by asking yourself: *how will you feel it 10 minutes from now? How about after 10 months? How about after 10*

years? Exercising yourself to ask these questions before executing a decision helps you eliminate emotion from influencing your decision. That is because you will force yourself to think about the long-term effects of your decisions. Emotions are catalysts that permit you to be biased with the decision that you are about to formulate.

3. ***The Outcome Blind Approach.*** You will always acquire inaccurate information, but you are always in control of your decisions and the processes that you are about to utilize in order to generate good decisions. If you are making a big decision, ask the input of the people who have involvement with the decision you have to make because they will be affected as well with the formulated decision. Always hold your ground whether your decision is a success or a

failure. By getting through both scenarios, you avoid **_attribution bias_** – judging others with their actions without giving consideration to the situation they are in. Applying this mental model gives you a high probability of making successful decisions because you don't allow any form of bias to affect your decision-making mechanism.

4. **_The Right and Non-Consensus._** The idea of this mental model is you have to be different and be bolder with your choices. This is quite risky, and yet very rewarding. In order to win, you have to be unconventional and be right at the same time. You have to muster all your strength and be positive all the time if you will apply this mental model.

5. **_The Rule of Three._** The rule of three is an effective writing principle that can actually work with your decisions.

Try to give three reasons, not two, not four, just three in persuading a client. Or you can also apply it when you are making your priority list. The lesser is much better for this principle.

6. **The Moat.** During the medieval era and the era directly succeeding it, a moat is a deep ditch filled with water that serves as the first line of defense of a castle, town, or fortress. No doubt that a moat diagram has been recreated and used in business as well. When you want to have a competitive edge and a powerful strategy, you can always utilize the moat and defend your business against competitors and win the game.

7. **The Combination of Network Effects and Critical Mass.** In order for you to expand your market and to reach the mass, you have to create a network. You need a medium to promote what you have to offer.

The fastest, easiest, and affordable way is through the use of social media. Of course, to effectively participate in the market, you have to learn your **critical mass** – it refers to the ideal size of your business.

8. ***Utilization of Decentralized, and Distributed Infrastructure.*** One of the essential factors in reaching an effective network impact is to create a distributed and decentralized model to balance the power between the company and the individuals.

9. ***The Famous Game Theory.*** How people behave in strategic situations is the primary concern of *game theory*. Being used by famous scientists and high-ranking officials, this mental model allows you to think of strategies where you can use your advantage to a maximum level and your competitors are reduced.

10. ***The Economies of Scale.*** They are cost advantages cultivated by businesses and other organizations when production becomes effective. It can be achieved by companies by having an increase in production and lowering the prices of the products. This is possible because prices are distributed over a large volume of products. Prices or costs can be fixed or variable. In this principle, the size of the business is the main factor because the larger it is, the more savings will be generated. It can also be external and internal. External deals with the outside elements, while internal is concerned with managerial factors. This model allows your business to grow faster without having a high fixed cost or overhead.

11. ***The Pyramid Principle.*** Under a thought, written ideas should always form a pyramid, and this is the

advocacy *pyramid principle*. To effectively use it, you must begin with the answer, group and summarize your underlying arguments, and finally put your supporting ideas in order. You should try this model when you are communicating or pitching a proposal. Start with the answer first instead of unveiling your agenda at the end of the presentation. So, you will allow your clients or the people you are dealing with to have their conclusions and get aligned with you. Also, you can save more time and effort.

12. ***The 99/50/1.*** If you dissect the numbers, you will get 99%, 50%, and 1% which actually denotes your commitment to a project. You have to be highly and physically involved at the beginning of the production and getting involved less if you secured its smooth transition until the final

phase. Utilizing this model will allow you to focus more on other tasks.

13. **_Become a Directly Responsible Individual (DRI)._** A concept that was highly adhered to by Apple, *DRI* is explicitly responsible for something, especially decisions. Being or having one lessens time and energy consumption during meetings and other scenarios. It always about efficiency and results and DRIs leave no space for vagueness on the issue of who has the authority and final say on every question that a project or team has. They should also be fully focused on their goals and tasks, as well as being open to collaboration in order to real success. They have the tendency to make all the final decisions but they should also learn how and when to trust the capability of their coworkers.

14. **_The Team of Teams._** This is an operating model that connects

together different teams as well as their members forming a network of an organization. Decision making is conducted by team leaders of each group making them responsible for success or failure. This model is a dramatic example of the proverb: *united we stand, divided we fall.*

15. ***The Radical Candor.*** Let's make this fast and simple, be an aggressive leader with an ultra-empathy to others. One of the most successful ways of becoming a great leader is by building positive relationships with your coworkers. You have to possess and be known as someone who is kind, genuine, reliably honest, and caring. If you cannot love your coworkers, it must be an indication that you cannot love your work for a longer time frame because of that manifestation. The atomic building block of good management is *honest*

feedback. There is nothing more destructive to a relationship than an imbalance of influence and power. The honest destroyer of truth that neutralizes this imbalance is **candor**. One more pointer, there is this thing called *ruinous empathy* or when you tend to care too much because of attachment that you have for some. To get past through it, you must identify that enjoying near-term empathy bypasses long-term impacts. You could lead your people to a bigger failure and more undesirable feelings in the future. Forgetting your true intention while you help people can be fatal and destructive for the business.

16. ***The Listen, Decide, Communicate Sequence.*** A communication model from Dick Costolo, the former CEO of Twitter, the *listen, decide, communicate sequence* is important in decision-

making. You have to listen first, if not to people, by the factors that you need to consider. Then you decide and communicate it with those involved.

Those mental models might not lead you to find necessary decisions easier, but it would definitely provide a clear platform for you to find success as a leader in progress. Since this chapter is dedicated to mental models, I have more latticework of models that you may use to optimize your results while spending less time and money. As you may observe, mental models are like handy applications you installed on your smartphone. You installed them because you know that they are helpful and fun. So, let me give you more applications that you can utilize.[5]

1. ***Regret Minimization Framework (Jeff Bezos).*** Jeff Bezos is a successful American entrepreneur and investor. He is famously known as the founder and president of Amazon.com,

Inc. –– one of the Big Four technology companies along with Google, Facebook, and Apple. *Regret minimization framework* allows you to make difficult decisions by visualizing your future and looking backward about your current decision. This mental model might help you fulfill your goal of building a business of your own or doing things that you are craving to do for a long time. Also, it will make you a risk taker and better try things and be optimistic that you will succeed. You might regret it if you don't give it a shot.

2. **Idea Maze (Balaji Srinivasan).** Balaji Srinivasan is the co-founder of Counsyl, a genetic test company that tells couples whether they are safe or not of having children. It has won the Wall Street Journal's Innovation Award for Medicine. This mental model is about thinking and planning

on different paths and detours your decision will take.

3. ***Schlep Blindness (Paul Graham).*** Paul Graham is an English computer scientist and entrepreneur who is best known for his work on Lisp – a high-level programming language that is used by different tech professionals around the globe. *Schlep* was a Yiddish word which means *a tedious and unpleasant work*. This mental model prevents you from overlooking possible risks of your decisions. It tells you that you must learn the things and cure your ignorance about a certain venture.

4. ***Jobs to be Done (Clayton Christensen).*** Clayton Christensen is an American academic and business consultant who is currently serving as a professor at the Harvard Business School. This mental model allows you to understand why a consumer may buy your product. With this, you can

accurately create and improve products that satisfy the need of your customers.

5. ***Minimum Viable Product (Frank Robinson).*** Frank Robinson was an American professional baseball player and manager in Major League Baseball. Throughout his career, he won the MVP on both American and National Leagues. *Minimum Viable Product*, a mental model formulated by a legendary MVP, is originally a process for trying assumptions and guarantees that there is a need for a certain idea. The MVP process starts by identifying your riskiest assumption. Then, knowing the simplest experiment that you can undertake to test that assumption.

6. **Please Keep in Mind: *Confirmation Bias of Thucydides.*** We have discussed *confirmation bias* in Chapter 2. As a recap, it is a form of thinking that you

agree with what confirms your assumptions and disagree with the opposing evidence. You have to avoid this type of thinking and be transparent because it doesn't get well with other models like the MVP and idea maze.

7. ***Product Market Fit (Andy Rachleff).*** Andy Rachleff is the founder and chairman of Wealthfront Inc. – an investment firm in California. *Product-market fit* is a model that puts you in good condition and your products satisfy your consumer.

8. ***100 People Love (Paul Graham).*** Good reviews and positive word-of-the-mouth-promotion are effective ways to propel your little business and be widely known. Paul Graham believes in this strategy of getting 100 people to love you and what you are promoting. From them, you build a network that expands to others until

your business acquires a stronghold in your industry. Advertisement from people who know you is cheaper than applying for an ad in radio, television, or publication. Also, social media platforms are out there for your disposal. So, you better have a list and write down if you got 100 people who love you personally.

9. **AARRR (Dave McClure).** Dave McClure is an entrepreneur and investor who founded the 500 Startups, a business accelerator company. *AARRR* stands for *Acquisition, Retention, Referral, Revenue* and it is a model for the customer lifecycle. It measures and optimizes each step of the funnel to grow rapidly and widen your market. It helps you also understand your consumers and a perfect tool for you to formulate a data-driven decision. And that is a powerful startup.

10. ***Network Effects (Robert Metcalfe).*** Robert Metcalfe is a tech-savvy, American entrepreneur and who co-invented the Ethernet and assisted the evolution of the internet. *Network effects* take place when a service or product increases its value as more consumers use it. This model also allows you to assemble a better business as you effectively strategize the market of your product or service.

11. ***Disruptive Innovation (Clayton Christensen).*** Ever wonder how the Billboard charts work? Billboard monitors the demands of albums and songs then ranks them according to their sales and streams. The *disruptive innovation* has the same concept. It is when you create a method, product, or service that is at the bottom of a market at first and relentlessly climbs up, outranking your competitors

because you are redefining the industry with what you can offer in the market.

12. ***Conjoined Triangles of Success (Jack Barker).*** A fictional main character in HBO's hit series Silicon Valley, Jack "Action" Barker shows us how ridiculous and thrilling startups can be. The *conjoined triangles of success* allow you to shape decisions by looking at every market of your success and avoid overlapping them because it might lead to your downfall. Gaining a unique perspective on reality between sales and engineering will give you an absolute edge in making wise decisions.

Aside from learning and applying different mental models in your every decision, I suggest that you must develop a system for your regular progress. In this specific section, I will teach you how to develop the systems which will definitely upgrade your way of thinking. And in order to make it happen, I will introduce to you another set of mental models from **systems thinking** which created the core to the approaches towards the success of many prominent figures. It is also a dynamic tool that can make improvements in all areas of your life possible. Possessing a big goal can stimulate you to act in order to achieve it, but only for a short period. You must remember that a system or process will always exceed your motivation.

A **system** as defined by Merriam-Webster Dictionary is a regularly interacting or interdependent group of items forming a unified whole. This unified whole is led to a definite objective. The system as a whole is greater than the sum of its components and can achieve more with better results. You take away a single component from the system that can lead to unpredictable changes. Everything in this world is a system. The best example is the universe and it consists of interacting components in which we are connected. We are an essential part of these many systems that exist in the universe and we are unique because we are constantly evolving. With our gift to think rationally, we can always emerge from the systems rather than being imprisoned to them. We can become the masters of the systems and formulate our own rules.

For you to be able to write your own rules in the infinite games of life, let me give you the vital mental models for systems thinking.

- ***Theory of Constraints.*** This mental model was developed from the realm of manufacturing systems. Every single system is reduced by different constraints but has one constraint which is tighter compared to the rest. Just like in a chain, there is always one weakest link and there will be a single weakest constraint in a system. This constraint is known as the **bottleneck** – the area where overwhelming congestion takes place that causes an interruption in a system. Its implication affects the performance of any system basically making it limited by the products that are coming out from the bottleneck. So, there must be an action that will address the bottleneck to see a gradual change, if not in an instant. This mental model opens our eyes to the reality that most of our ways of self-improvement are fruitless because of our failure to recognize their bottlenecks. We find ourselves in the middle of the ocean, floating and swimming but not getting ashore. You have to remember that you don't need more labor, but efforts that are applied effectively. You have to focus on removing your bottleneck and ignore the others for the meantime. Once it is removed, your system will smoothly run as it should be, and you will feel a big change in your life.

- ***Having concrete leverage.*** You've got to have leverage in order to influence your system positively and in a way that your efforts will have maximum effect. Leverage is the answer to your limited time, focus, and energy. Having it, you can fully maximize your return of investment from your resources. Beginning leaders use willpower to create motivation while professionals use it for fortifying their systems of execution. The **Pareto Principle**, also known as the 80/20 rule, states that it is on the power-law distribution where the majority of the phenomena fall. It also adheres that 80% of the outcomes can be attained using 20% of the effort which is not actually impressive. Why is this so? Because you can have 50% of the outcomes by just using 1% effort. This fact wants to imply that you must understand the level of expertise or skill your objective is requiring you before you undergo diminishing marginal returns. You really have to choose your areas of mastery to equip yourself better. Your leverage tells you the opportunities in small changes in your life that might lead to expanded success. To better improve and maximize the power of your leverage, you have to use the following approach in your systems.

- You have to **change the rules** so you can define what to do within your system.
- You can design and customize your own systems **build in self-organization**. This way, they will naturally improve as time goes by.
- You must **improve your information flow** by making more objective and accurate measurements by

frequently checking on them. Reflecting regularly on information gained from the measurements will improve your systems.

- ***Getting Feedback.*** The distribution and returning of information to a system are called ***feedback***. Its primary function is to inform the system about its status relative to the goal. Feedback is like a loop because the connection between the measurement and the factor that is being measured is circular. Feedback is very vital to the system because of the information they hold if the measurements are getting closer to the desired outcome. Feedback is creating a loop that affects the overall system. We have two types of feedback loops. First is the ***balancing feedback loop*** which is the most common and it tries to stabilize the equilibrium or status quo. The second is the ***reinforcing feedback loop*** which delivers growth (+) or decline (−) to a system. You need feedback loops to keep your most wanted outcomes stable and minimize the setbacks when you lose your way towards your goal. You have to be vigilant in balancing feedback loops. Counterbalancing it will cause delays and problems in achieving what you desire.

-

The additional mental models above are very powerful when you combine together because they form a mechanism for advancement. You are now aware that measurement and awareness are vital keeps for you to learn how to overcome any obstacles that are halting you in reaching your goals. It is also important that you have to undertake minor behavioral experiments to clarify your assumptions. One tiny problem might change everything else, but identifying your bottlenecks allows you to be well prepared.

Giving your full attention, time, and energy in fixing your bottlenecks, with the help of your leverage, will make your productivity fast and smooth over time. Be vigilant for all the time and observe for samples in your everyday existence and use them as a reference. Once you fully understand the nature of every system, you will begin to see it everywhere.

The more references that you have, you will also begin to form many ideas for enhancement that are not connected to your bottlenecks anymore. I would like you to try this, find one bottleneck that is limiting you now, focus on how you would fix it...without thinking about your other bottlenecks. Problems are a lot easier to solve one at a time so you won't feel stressed in the process.

Digging More About Mental Models

Imagine that you are in a garden one sunny morning, then it suddenly rains. You look at the falling droplets, you feel them on your skin. As you are observing, the lenses of your eyes concentrate photons from the light emitted by the sun into your retinas. There are photosensitive cells residing in your retinas that respond by distributing neural impulses to the brain. The brain works on these signals and creates an image of the rain in your head. That's the scientific explanation of how images of things you see form in your brain. The question is, what makes the picture of the rain an authentic one? This is how we use the **mental model**. The rain is an idea that really exists in reality and that is the model right in front of you. It is what you see and what you feel as of the moment. Understanding the model is demanding more information aside from your sensory experience. You can use information from your experiences and education.

Rain is defined as water in the form of droplets caused by the condensation of water vapor. It can be predicted and can occur seasonally. It is vital for drylands and plants, especially in farms where rice fields and other crops grow. You are confident by those facts that are related to the rain because you got the basic knowledge about it and the weather patterns remind you of it. Mental models are packed with knowledge that can also help you create other ideas.

More About Systems

Our brain is great at simulating mental models for our instant form of reality. Factors are getting difficult when you begin to think about the abstract. The best example that we can use for the abstract system in the market. The market system has products that which value is determined by their price. This price acts as a signal if a consumer can afford the product. Unlike our first sample, the rain, you cannot see the market physically. Obviously, the market is an abstract idea that lives in the minds of people who patronize it. There was an overwhelming economic crisis in late 2008, before the holiday shopping season. It was when retailers struggled financially due to the rapid decline of consumer purchases. People were troubled about the economy that they started saving money instead of spending it. In order to boost demand, retailers started dropping prices of their commodities. This option led to *price deflation*. Consumers observed the pattern of rapid price drop resulting in delayed spending and waiting for commodities to drop their value. This result of simulating the consumers' mental models of the market affected their decision-making that the more they delay buying, the cheaper the commodities would be.

It is difficult to describe the boundaries of a mental model. We are capable of narrowing our concentration and work on temporary facts within the scope of our mental models. Also, we are not good enough at mentally processing complex systems with lots of parts, variables, and interruptions. This is when we need to use the software. With software, we can change the state of our mental models into functional models. It also aids us in creating new knowledge and perception, as well as to build better mental models in the coming situations.

Pareto Principle

We have discussed this mental model earlier and as a recap, it is also known as ***80/20 principle*** which is a form of ***power-law*** –– a special mathematical connection between two variables in which one works as the power of the other. The *Pareto Principle* states that 20% of a set of factors pave the way for 80% of the outcomes. Anyway, it doesn't always have to be 80/20, it can also be 25/95 or 5/70. As you may observe, they don't always have to be summed up to 100%. This principle tells the idea that many causes and cases are not linear in nature, the small percentage of causes result in the majority of the effects. There are many simple examples of this principle like 20% of consumers can generate 80% of the revenue.

This mental model can be utilized if you can find out the main motivators for a specific effect that you are able to observe, then you optimize it for more promising outcomes. In a typical work setting, there are tasks or projects that are valuable to a company or a boss. By identifying them, you can focus on them and do your best. By doing so, you have a chance to be promoted or your presence be felt in the company. Charlie Munger is one of the most successful investors who utilized this principle and according to him, it does the heavy lifting and only a few mental models he had known can do such a thing.

Law of Small Numbers

This concept is part of probability which tells that you will witness the majority of variation in small samples. Obviously, it is the opposite of the *Law of Large Numbers* which discusses that the real probability will come out using a large number of samples. The main idea of the **law of small numbers** is that a small portion of samples will have outcomes that have many variations which can also be misleading.

The best example that we use is the performance of a specific school. Many people would give an assumption that schools with small population tend to perform better than those that are bigger. But in reality, they can also be the worst performers. It is easy to see that having a small number can propel a school's ranking by selecting the best through entrance examinations and removal of students who don't reach the average required in a specific program. This action can definitely propel a school's ranking against its bigger competitors. While there are several small schools which are parts of smaller communities and don't require anything in accepting students. If you see in the research in 2018 by a member of the National Association for College Admission Counseling, where they listed the 100 top-performing public schools in the United States, there are smaller schools in the top and bottom of the list.[10] The sample population in smaller schools are not large enough to measure the quality of education of the school in a specific time frame. By using the law of small numbers in ranking the schools, it would be easy for parents to put their children in the best schools if they want to have a quality education. In the corporate world, this mental model is the reason why Charlie Munger quoted that personal interviews as a classic medium of the hiring process are a terrible way. He suggested that it is best to look at the applicant's portfolio and qualifications. Munger believes that interviews have a sample size of one and a bad indicator of how the applicant will perform at the posted job or how he will communicate with other employees.

This mental model is highly associated and directly inclined to probability and can also have harmony with other mental models. It can lead to overconfidence and to huge losses when it is paired with *leverage*. There are random events that may happen all the time and when a business or a businessman decides to borrow resources from other corporations to support growth, they have the mentality that things will stay as long as they are paying their debt. The same concept is the main motivation for *redundancy* in engineering –– adding backups to the systems to survive possible setbacks.

The Circle of Competence

Having an awareness of your circle of competence gives you the power to avoid problems, recognize opportunities for growth, and to accept learning from others. The idea of the circle of competence has been utilized for so many years by Warren Buffet as a path to concentrate investors on working in areas they have mastered. Learning the boundaries of your capacity is essential. This mental model has a very simple concept. Every one of us has amassed helpful information in certain realms of the world through learning and experience. Some of these realms are very easy for us to understand, while other areas need more intelligence or information to be fully understood. Like in school, there are subjects that we love the most because we excel in them. We hate or we get bored with some of these bodies of knowledge because we have a hard time understanding their concept. Buffet believed that we do not need to gain a full understanding of the areas we have a hard time comprehending. We have to stick to the things that we really know. Our circle of competence can become broader as time goes by. Always remember that in order for us to learn more, we have to accept the errors. Surely, we will commit mistakes along the process and learn from them. Unless you are a perfect creature.

If you want to improve your chances of becoming a successful person in life and as a leader or entrepreneur, then identify the scope of your circle of competence and work hard inside. As time goes by, do your best to expand your circle but never, ever be afraid to accept your limitations.

More, more mental models...

I have given you several proven and tested mental models and I would like you to know that I am not done yet in giving you more for you to utilize and experiment as you make day-to-day decisions. Indulge the list again!

- ***Checklist*** – it is a tool that you can utilize to form a list or outline the things that you need to accomplish. It will help you to set your priorities and also will serve as a remember since your memory is limited. A checklist also increases your consistency and accuracy by providing you the proper sequence of repetitive processes.

- ***Advantages of Scale*** – it refers to the concept that as a system works more of the same kind of task, it will achieve efficiencies after a long time. There is a greater range of efficiencies that can be acquired as business flourishes such as employees getting better at their tasks which leads the way to meet deadlines ahead of time.

- ***Redundancy*** – it is originally a model from engineering which refers to the methods of allowing extra parts within a system. They act as substitutes or backups that can be utilized once a part is broken so the system continues to function and to avoid delay. Therefore, redundancy is very important within a system because it reduces the chance of system failure.

- ***Division of Labor*** – is a model that allows each person without an organization to specialize in different tasks or skills. Once a specific skill or process has been mastered, everyone can share the knowledge learned to provide growth and efficiency not just to the organization, but as well as to its members.
- ***Incentives*** – also known as ***rewards*** is a strategy that you can use to motivate your people. By providing people with the incentives that they deserve, you can change their behavior and reach for the goal that you have in mind.

Chapter 5 – Negotiation and How to Make it a Win-Win

In the previous chapters, you have learned how powerful mental models can affect your decision-making and predict the long-term effects of your decisions with thorough contemplation and scientific analysis. There are so many mental models and I know that you have observed that they are not just for decision-making, but to sort your priorities in life and to make successful methods that will help you find success. Mental models are giving you tactics and pointers on how to make effective negotiations and powerful persuasion. If you are dreaming of a business of your own or winning deals that will put you on the pedestal, it is vital for you to learn things on how to master the art of negotiation and persuasion.

One of the most common errors that business negotiators or managers commit is rushing into a proposal without enough preparation. In order to create strong arguments and persuasive clauses, you need ample time to study the content of what you are doing. Because of ambition and taking shortcuts to be recognized, negotiators and managers are prone to create unreasonable demands and other dirty tactics to win deals. You always have to see room for improvement and always have an open mind for collaboration. A flashy bonus is a good motivator, but being a good leader, you must think not just your own sake but for the betterment of those people who are looking up to you. Emotions play a very important factor in making negotiations and proposals. Negotiators and managers are not able to do their best once they let emotional biases get into their way. Anger and sadness can lead to risky and unhealthy decisions. They are also prone to ethical shortcuts and behave unethically during negotiations because of financial incentives because of the mentality that they are already experts in their respective fields and won't be caught in doing anomalies.

Yes, most of the mistakes that you will encounter, or you have encountered already as a leader, negotiator, or manager, root from your dark side. I fully understand that because our nature says that we are *innately good and innately evil*. We tend to do things, in case you have, against our moral code because we are in a situation, or because of the success it can bring, or whatever reasons, we must avoid it at all costs. Once you did something that you think will never be uncovered, it is like a drug, very addictive and it will consume you until you lose control. I strongly believe in the *law of karma* and I must say that you must live in the golden rule, "*do not do unto others what you don't want others to do unto you.*"

Robert Cialdini and the Influence: The Psychology of Persuasion

Robert Cialdini is the celebrated author of the best-selling book entitled *Influence: The Psychology of Persuasion*. He is a professor and a social psychologist who has conducted complex and important research -- making him the most cited expert in the psychology of negotiation, influence, and persuasion. Cialdini introduced in his book the **six universal principles of influence** which are also called the *six weapons of influence*. Since its publication 35 years ago, the concepts from the book are still in use by businesses and organizations around the globe.

The creation of the book began with the author's theoretical perspective to deal with a complicated world, our brains evolved fluidly, and we respond to different situations. The six principles revolve primarily on human instincts. Other ordinary circumstances are good traits but can be utilized against us by those who want to destroy or control us. The author was hoping by understanding these principles of persuasion, we are better to identify events where they will act against their influence and to have the shield to fight undesirable social impact.

The first principle is **reciprocity** which states that individuals always want to return favors, pay debts, and to be kind to others who showed kindness as well. These samples are leading to the conclusion that we always tend to say *yes*. It is already a cultural standard that we have to return gifts and favors. This principle tells that people feel that they owe people who something good to them. People tend to feel uncomfortable when they are indebted to others. So, they will find ways to *reciprocate* the good deeds, just to satisfy or lessen the weight of obligation. This principle can also be utilized for unexpected exchanges as well. Its occurrence affected our ability to decide without restrictions and led us to respond involuntarily or automatically. To defend yourself from reciprocity, you must reject the offers. If you see offers as tricks or bait to control you, then you don't have to be obligated to reciprocate that offer. Unless you know that you can trust the person who offered and see meaningful exchanges. Always remember that you are the captain of your own ship and you can always decline to avoid reciprocity.

The second principle is ***commitment and consistency*** where the author argues that people have a longing to be consistent and they also value consistency from other things. It is a powerful social influence and highly valued by our society. Its principle suggests that we have an urge to be acknowledged as consistent and that we honor our commitments. Once we give our commitment to someone or to something, we are doing our best to keep our end of the bargain. Like we support projects that have an appeal to us. For Cialdini, commitments are very powerful to influence someone who is motivated or uncorrupted by power. To fight this principle, you have to stay cool and do not be pressured by accommodating requests that you really don't want to be involved in. You have to identify personal signals that can you help the right decisions.

The third principle talks about safety in considering numbers or the wisdom of the masses – the concept of **social proof**. Because of uncertainties or doubts that we have in making decisions, we seek validation for our actions from people. It is like you want to drink milk tea and you want the best-tasting store, you will conduct your own research to find the best shop where many people buy and generally have positive reviews from its customers. You have to be very careful in looking into others because you might be following a questionable person. It is vital for you to identify that the actions of others should not be the absolute basis of your decisions.

The fourth principle is the acceptance of **authority**. We have been taught since we were young that we need to comply with the demands of people who have power over us and respect them as well. Then, as we mature, we want to be like the people that we admired the most because of their influence. Sometimes, we are blinded by titles, possessions, and fiscal outlook that we forget to look for a true substance. There are authorities who abused their influence and power. In order for you to protect yourself, ask first if a person of considerable status has triggered your respect for authority genuinely and not because they imposed the power of their symbol.

Cialdini believes that we are more likely to be influenced by people we like –– and the fifth principle talks about **liking**. If we like the person who asks for a favor, admit it, we are more than happy and willing to be at that person's disposal. We feel that we are needed, and we can use and go back to the first principle, reciprocity. Cialdini enumerated factors why we are inclined to like a person. It might be because of appearance, influence, social circle, commonality, and flattery. Someone may compliment you when they want something from you. To counter this and for you not to be used by people who want to take advantage, you must learn how to separate emotional attachments and focus more on the weight of the favor. Assess the favor if you or others would benefit from it. Even if you like the person, you still have to be extra careful and be transparent.

The last and the sixth principle is the **scarcity** which is super powerful and works on the worth that individuals apply to things. Scarcity in economics is connected to supply and demand. The rarer the item is, the more valuable it can become, and people have the mentality to want it. The author exerts that people are defied emotionally when their freedoms are endangered, and scarcity has the tendency to limit free choice. It may cause people to want to have possession of the item. People find opportunities valuable when they are actually less valuable. It is a lesson that you must incorporate into your life; you must analyze the item, or an opportunity before you take it. Ask yourself what kind of value you would get and reflect on its long-term effect.

Referrals

- ***Social Proof*** We have already discussed this principle which is part of the book of the famous psychologist Robert Cialdini. Let us find out more about ***social proof***. Social proof is a form of cognitive bias that defines how we are greatly persuaded by what the people around us are practicing. It is sometimes called as Herd Mentality, it is a kind of shortcut (heuristic) where we depend big time on the ideas and acts of the people around us, especially when we are creating a decision. This possibility is more likely to materialize when we are clouded with uncertainties. In any event, especially when you are stressed or confused, you tend to look for the crowd and seek confirmation from the majority. Social proof is one of the most utilized and effective tools if you want to persuade a person and influence their decisions. Salespeople are very good at it. So, if you are inclined corporately, you must learn the tricks of this cognitive bias. It can also be combined with other mental models like **authority** or you can also partner it with **scarcity** to create unusual patterns such as sell-offs and bank runs.

- ***Getting to Yes*** It is a book based on the efforts of the Harvard Negotiation Project, *Getting to Yes* is a good material on effective negotiation that leads both parties in a win-win situation. This book also thoughtfully combined different mental models, transforming them into a very beneficial discussion of how to reach winning solutions when problems emerge. Primarily more on business and professional discussions, there are pointers that you can use in personal matters too. It contains practical, concise, and applicable content and gives thoughtful solutions for a lot of issues.

It is not actually a good idea to eliminate conflict because it can actually lead to better opportunities. We can actually prevent it by altering our ways and work on our differences. Like, collaborate and transform that collaboration to win-win situations instead of proving who's the best. We have to focus more on interests rather than positions — for example, a landowner and a tenant. The tenant rents land and pays rent regularly. To maximize the rented land, the landowner allows the tenant to build a business that would boost the tenant's income. It is a win-win situation where the landowner is getting rental payments from the tenant while the latter is earning and is able to pay rentals in advance because of the business he builds. Different interests or having different utility functions can pave the way to **mutual gain** – this is the foundation of capitalism. So, you better hold and prevent your confirmation bias in getting your way to have a mutual understanding and harmony with your collaborator.

Traditional negotiation can be classified as *soft* or *hard* and both have their own downsides. Practically, the hard one dominates the soft, but being too hard can really be exhausting and suffocating. A principled negotiation is an approach where the one proposing separates people from the conflict, concentrates on interests and not for positions, formulates choices for common growth, and asserts on utilizing objective criteria. Always remember that when you deal, you must have empathy and deal with the interest of the other party. Failing to build rapport can also lead to the dismissal of the negotiation. You should proactively bring out some emotions. Be confident when you are pitching because conflict exists not in physical reality, but in your head. You need to deal and overcome your fears like feeling inferior or building pessimistic thoughts which include rejection. Do not blame others for your personal issues and you must solve it on your own or you could ask for help from the people who care for you. There are certain issues that might be unimportant for you but meaningful for others. Therefore, if you have business issues, allow your people to help by joining the process because no matter what the outcome is, they will be happy because they felt needed. The success of their production will give them happiness and they will see failure as a room for great improvements.

There are moments when people around you feel exhaustion and emotional stress. You always have to display empathy and be very welcome to their anger. Venting out is a good choice if you want to loosen up. If other people attack you, be silent and do not respond to show how professional you are. You have to be open to criticisms because harsh comments can give you the motivation to work harder and prove to those people who are letting you down that you are not the person that they are projecting just to mock you. Sometimes, you can conduct an interview and ask people about the areas that need further improvement. Through this, you are becoming an effective leader because you need to learn more about the welfare of those who are working with you. You need to negotiate under legal circumstances and do not undertake illegal things like using dirty tricks just to get what they want from you.

- ***The Humans vs. Econs Mental Model*** One of the most common bottlenecks that we have around is that we often see things in accordance with our perspective, or the way we desire them to be. That is a very inconvenient habit because our surroundings are changing in forms or events that we don't expect. So, you have to pattern your life to accommodate reality itself. Humans are "us", so what about **econs**? Well, it simply refers to **economics** and **economists**. We already have a clue all along. Econs are doing their best to get incentives and be motivated by it and boost their interests. While normal humans always value fairness and rely heavily on social proof. They have the tendency to take away what is rightfully theirs to return a favor or to show consistency. But they can also be destructive when someone wronged them, or they are being threatened by an unfair and unjust system. We can put that it is the critical point of negotiation.

Humans, not econs, are the foundation of the *human-centered design approach* or *structural problem-solving*. This approach asserts that you cannot expect people around you to behave the way you want them to behave. Expect them to behave the way they want instead. Various professionals like lawyers, engineers, scientists, and people in the business world are trying to control things based on their designs simply because they are too analytical and imagine the things around them as the same. These professionals are like econs because of their education and they lean on the concept of sunk and opportunity costs. Such a concept can blind leaders and ignore human interests like fairness or memory that can lead to theoretical systems that don't work in reality. The most common complaint of leaders of big corporations about investors is they see companies as disorganized cash machines moving on spreadsheets rather than actual living things that breathe vital entities and facing standard human challenges. You might fail to consider the loss aversion, fairness, endowment effect, and self-justification – you have to see that people tend to overvalue their possessions and as time goes by, they feel entitled and boast what they have no matter what their sources are. There are so many business people and investors who are focusing so much on the records of their spreadsheets. Incentives, in reality, are complicated topics to be discussed and well-understood human psychology provides a more accurate solution.

One of the most overlooked mental models is **local vs. globalization** that tells the idea that decisions that are created for the short-term are not applicable in the long-term and vice versa. It is always present in businesses and badly dealt with. Most managers can adopt cost-saving materials because it is a rational decision, but they tend to see human needs and invoke fairness in any given circumstance. Loss aversion is being applied when businesses put fairness by applying discounts to their products and sacrificing whopping profits that they could gain.

Business managers who are already a veteran in their fields can have mercy and give in to human needs by applying discounts and prioritize fairness and other concerns therein for a long-term harmony between profit and consumers' approval. While most human traits should be considered as adaptive and like water, they do follow the shape of the frame created in the economy.

- ***Reason Respecting*** The word ***because*** is one of the most powerful words in the English language. As humans, we were given the capacity to think and to reason out which separate us from other life forms. Our intellect allows us to inquire about the things we don't know. Our inquisition gives way to the concept that we have to understand the reasons for everything in this universe. When we learn the answers to our why's, we are willing to comply, to remember, and to finish an order successfully. **Because** is a powerful motivator or tool for persuasion for both positive and negative goals.

One basic scenario that we can observe by utilizing the powerful effect of "because" is when you are falling in line. So, it is common that when there is a long line, some are patiently waiting while others are irritated because of what it seems to be a very long time for waiting. Then, there are individuals who have special cases that will use their status or situation like pregnancy, old age, and disabilities and cut into the line. Since they have a "because" or valid reason, anyone who is perfectly normal accepts the reason and understands the situation. Or, in the business world, you have to act professionally and be presentable all the time "*because*" they are part of the company rules that you must abide.

Because is a very potent word as you can persuade people to do things that you want, whether they are good or bad, and they can do the same for you. In a corporate setup, when you have a project and you have to finish it urgently, by simply explaining *why* this project is vital to your company and *why* you have to finish it urgently, you can influence that willingness to your coworkers pushing them to focus and finish the project. If you also want an increase, use *because* and write down detailed information on the important tasks or projects you completed, include your performance and functions, and how you made an impact on your company. You can also use the word to adapt to right-hand issues to solve them.

Every professional, even the average person, is always looking for reasons and *reason-respecting* is a cognitive bias and a persuasion tactic at the same time. By simply adding *because* to different media like verbal communication or email, it will increase the chances that your request will be granted, or people will comply with what you want. To add more, adding the question of *why* when you need a certain thing like a project to be done in time can help your resources to focus and do their best to adapt along the process.

So, the use of the words *because* and *why* will help you to meet your goals and influence people within your circle to actively and willingly participate in your demand as long as you have the will and goals to achieve. Reasons are very important because it is a validation and a form of justification of where efforts and resources will be used.

In using mental models, you have to recognize the issues and problems before you use them. There are always at your disposal, but you must be careful because you may use the wrong one or the wrong combination. Anyway, for what I have mentioned for so many times, it is okay to fail because utilizing mental models on the wrong occasion will let you know where it is best suited. Do not be afraid to experiment because it will lead you to better opportunities. You just have to be optimistic and find what is best suited to your system.

You can also develop your own mental models over time, especially when you are already leading. Part of leadership is the obstacles that you have to conquer and find what your strengths and weaknesses are, and where you have to be hard or soft. Be empathic in with the people around you and share a part of you that will empower them. Showing how human you are despite your achievements and position will definitely make a mark to the people that you shared a part of you. Be a great inspiration and always do legal things no matter how much you can make. Always believe in the *law of karma.* Find opportunities in every collaboration because it will bring harmony as you achieve your goals. You must allow others to participate to let them feel that they are wanted. Finishing a project through group effort, you are giving every single member self-worth. Every entity in the universe will conspire and will give you what you truly deserve. You can be hard on people who will trick you or those who tricked you already but be smart enough on plotting against them and make it sure that they will learn the lesson that they deserve. Through this, they might learn not to victimize others.

Let your system be in perfect harmony and work on first with your bottlenecks to guarantee a smooth-sailing business. Do not forget the maintenance of your system and install concepts that will keep it running towards your goals. Learning the business that you will work on and mastering the art of effective negotiation by providing powerful proposals leads to your success and the success of the people involved with it.

And when you reach all your goals, be grounded and do not forget to look back and thank the people who help you achieve your goals. Always believe in yourself and be confident. Be bolder with your choices and be different because you have to believe that you are a trendsetter.

Your decisions define you as a leader. Mental models are always there to help you out. Be analytic and review things that will lead you on the winning side. Optimism and letting others help you as long as you consider their merits increase the chances that you will generate the best decisions.

Conclusion

This book is created to help you analyze factors and construct wise decisions using mental models. To be a part of your start, or to be applied in your growing endeavor, is a great thing because it means that the purpose of this book has been greatly satisfied. Unlocking your mental abilities to explore what you think is impossible with the help of different concepts and methods written in this book equates to your long-term growth.

There might be concepts in this book that are new to you and I know that it is fun to experience new things, while it could be the opposite for others. You have to practice working on them so you can see their full potential and apply them to the most suitable situations. Exploring the different mental models will tell you where and when they are most suited.

The way in accumulating various mental models is like fortifying your eyesight by supplying your system with vitamin A. Our eyes can see something deeper in the surface. You need them together to have a better vision of things. Try to cover one of them, and you will have a very limited view. It is similar to mental models – they provide an abstract figure of how physical and theoretical things work in this universe. You should always be alert and vigilant in your surroundings so you can have pointers and improve the way you see things. Read often, learn from other people, and gather experience from important events in your life. The mind is essentially in need of different mental models to have a complete understanding of how the world works. The more references that you have, the more you open your mind with possibilities. Remember that the archenemy of good decisions is an insufficient understanding of the real problem.

During our academic pursuit, we have learned different areas of knowledge like mathematics, science, history, and so on. In practical application, information is not often segregated into different categories. As quoted by Charlie Munger, all the wisdom in this world is not found in one tiny academic faculty. Philosophers and other thinkers are free thinkers which means that they do not actually think based on a specific discipline. They acquire practical and personal wisdom of things that also work for them personally. They are trying their best to look at things not just in a single context. So, you have to consider other perspectives about a specific subject and develop flexible knowledge that can be connected from one idea to another. That is the importance of learning mental models, by learning how to relate them with each other for you to generate good decisions. You have to be creative and innovative in concluding your own ideas. Spotting the connection between different mental models, you can recognize answers to several questions that other people are overlooking.

You have to keep on reminding yourself that it is not necessary to gain mastery in every subject in order to gain a great decision-making mechanism. Of all the existing mental models that have existed in history, created and developed from the ancient times up to the present generation, there are only a few that you have to master and understand fully and work in combinations to see how the universe works. Most of the important mental models are large ideas from all disciplines like math, science, psychology, philosophy and the like. Each of them has a selection of mental models that create the spine of the subject. Like in science, we have learned experimentation, the theory of relativity and game theory to name a few that we may also apply in decision-making. If you are able to gain fluency in the ***foundations*** and the ***basics*** of every existing discipline, you can definitely acquire an extraordinarily precise and helpful image of life. Once again, according to Charlie Munger, 80 or 90 essential models will handle about 90 percent of the journey in transforming you as an effective decision-maker. And from those mental models, only a few would last and endure the weight of the journey. It is best if you could make it a personal mission to dismantle the great models that lift heavy factors of life. After you've learned more than a thousand different mental models, slowly try to select a few that really work.

I hope that you would create your personal list of the most essential and memorable mental models that you have already applied in various situations in your personal and corporate life. Also, give it a try to explain and remember their actual application. Explain to them in an easy and meaningful way to perceive by everyone. Make it your goal to share your experiences with mental models and help everyone within your social circle the way you help yourself to think and make decisions much better.

If you want to learn more about effective and helpful leadership strategies, please grab your copy of Emotional Intelligence for Leadership: 4 Week Booster Plan to Increase Your Self-Awareness, Assertiveness and Your Ability to Manage People written by yours truly, Jonatan Slane.

References

1. Weinschenk, S. (2019, February 7). How People Make Decisions. Retrieved August 12, 2019, from https://www.smashingmagazine.com/2019/02/human-decision-making/.
2. Soon, Chun & Brass, Marcel & Heinze, Hans-Jochen & Haynes, John-Dylan. (2008). Unconscious determinants of free decisions in the human brain. Nature neuroscience. 11. 543-5. 10.1038/nn.2112.
3. Adams, S. (2019, February 17). The Spanish Armada. Retrieved August 19, 2017, from http://www.bbc.co.uk/history/british/tudors/adams_armada_01.shtml.
4. History.com Editors. (2010, February 9). Spanish Armada defeated. Retrieved August 19, 2019, from https://www.history.com/this-day-in-history/spanish-armada-defeated.

5. Foroux, D. (2018, September 13). Mental Models and Making Decisions You Don't Regret. Retrieved August 7, 2019, from https://dariusforoux.com/mental-models/.
6. Rana, Z. (2017, September 7). Charlie Munger: How to Get Smarter by Using Mental Models. Retrieved August 19, 2019, from https://fs.blog/charlie-munger/.
7. Chen, J. (2019, June 25). Charlie Munger. Retrieved August 19, 2019, from https://www.investopedia.com/terms/c/charlie-munger.asp.
8. Heshmat, S. (2015, April 23). What Is Confirmation Bias? Retrieved August 22, 2019, from https://www.psychologytoday.com/us/blog/science-choice/201504/what-is-confirmation-bias.
9. Lewis, S. (1995). Alfred Korzybski. Retrieved September 4, 2019, from http://stevenlewis.info/gs/akbio.htm.

10. Wahba, P. (2015, March 13). Apple extends lead in the U.S. top 10 retailers by sales per square foot. Retrieved September 5, 2019, from https://fortune.com/2015/03/13/apples-holiday-top-10-retailers-iphone/.
11. History of mobile phones and the first mobile phone. (2019, February 21). Retrieved September 8, 2019, from https://www.uswitch.com/mobiles/guides/history-of-mobile-phones/.
12. Sincero, S. M. (2013, August 1). Selective Perception. Retrieved September 8, 2019, from https://explorable.com/selective-perception.
13. Stimulus [Def. 5]. (n.d.). In Dictionary.com, Retrieved September 8, 2019, from https://www.dictionary.com/browse/stimuli.
14. Chabris, C., & Simons, D. (n.d.). The Invisible Gorilla. Retrieved September 9, 2019, from

http://www.theinvisiblegorilla.com/gorilla_experiment.html.
15. Burrowes, R. J. (2016, July 17). The Psychology of Ideology and Religion. Retrieved September 10, 2019, from http://www.ipsnews.net/2016/07/the-psychology-of-ideology-and-religion/.
16. Kolbert, E. (2008, February 17). What was I thinking. Retrieved September 9, 2019, from https://www.newyorker.com/magazine/2008/02/25/what-was-i-thinking.
17. Forbes Coaches Council. (2018, June 4). Learning from Mistakes: 10 Things Beginning Leaders Should Know. Retrieved September 10, 2019, from https://www.forbes.com/sites/forbescoachescouncil/2018/06/04/learning-from-mistakes-10-things-beginning-leaders-should-know/#fe0ee47235b0.
18. Farnam Street. (n.d.). First Principles: The Building Blocks of True Knowledge.

Retrieved September 10, 2019, from https://fs.blog/2018/04/first-principles/.

19. Farnam Street. (n.d.). Thought Experiment: How Einstein Solved Difficult Problems. Retrieved September 11, 2019, from https://fs.blog/2017/06/thought-experiment-how-einstein-solved-difficult-problems/.

20. Farnam Street. (n.d.). Second-Order Thinking: What Smart People Use to Outperform. Retrieved September 10, 2019, from https://fs.blog/2016/04/second-order-thinking/.

21. Hayes II, J. (2018, September 29). 1 Powerful but Simple Technique Ray Dalio Uses to Make Better Decisions. Retrieved September 2019, from https://www.inc.com/julian-hayes-ii/ray-dalios-technique-to-instantly-becoming-a-better-decision-maker-boils-down-to-8-words.html.

22. Farnam Street. (n.d.). The Value of Probabilistic Thinking: Spies, Crime, and Lightning Strikes. Retrieved September 2019, from https://fs.blog/2018/05/probabilistic-thinking/.
23. Muñoz, S. (2018, October 24). Mental Models for Product Managers: The Inversion Principle. Retrieved September 11, 2019, from https://medium.com/@simonmunoz/mental-models-for-product-managers-the-inversion-principle-4f7692bddc2.
24. SUNK COSTS / COMMITMENT + CONSISTENCY BIAS MENTAL MODEL (INCL THESIS DRIFT). (n.d.). Retrieved September 12, 2019, from http://www.askeladdencapital.com/sunk-costs-commitment-consistency-bias-mental-model-incl-thesis-drift/.
25. PRODUCT VS. PACKAGING / ACTION BIAS MENTAL MODEL (INCL PRECISION VS. ACCURACY, BUSYNESS

VS. PRODUCTIVITY). (n.d.). Retrieved September 12, 2019, from http://www.askeladdencapital.com/product-vs-packaging-action-bias-mental-model-incl-precision-vs-accuracy-busyness-vs-productivity/
26. Tuck. (2019, July 20). Chronotypes. Retrieved September 12, 2019, from https://www.tuck.com/chronotypes/.
27. McVagh, Andrew. (2018, August 7). Mental Model Summary: Base Rates. Retrieved September 12, 2019, from https://www.mymentalmodels.info/mms-base-rates/.
28. Pressure [Def. 1]. (n.d.). In Merriam-Webster, Retrieved September 13, 2019, from https://www.merriam-webster.com/dictionary/pressure.
29. Center for Creative Leadership. (2019). The #1 Reason You Are Stressed and How to Change It. Retrieved September 13, 2019, from https://www.ccl.org/articles/leading-

effectively-articles/banish-stress-stop-ruminating/.
30. Bonnevalle, N. (2018, October 10). Leaders should care about mental health (including their own). Retrieved September 13, 2019, from https://medium.com/thnk-school-of-creative-leadership/leaders-should-care-about-mental-health-including-their-own-4c8ab9a4a57b.
31. Karnjanaprakorn, M. (2017, May 23). 16 Mental Models for Founders and Leaders. Retrieved September 13, 2019, from https://medium.com/personal-growth/16-mental-models-for-founders-and-leaders-25c3724a5208.
32. Hoffman, Jayme. (2016, May 21). 13 Mental Models Every Founder Should Know. Retrieved September 15, 2019, from https://medium.com/the-mission/13-mental-models-every-founder-should-know-c4d44afdcdd.

33. System [Def. 1]. (n.d.). In Merriam-Webster, Retrieved September 15, 2019, from https://www.merriam-webster.com/dictionary/pressure.
34. Sparks, C. (2017, August 15). 104: Systems Thinking — The Essential Mental Models Needed for Growth. Retrieved September 15, 2019, from https://medium.com/@SparksRemarks/systems-thinking-the-essential-mental-models-needed-for-growth-5d3e7f93b420.
35. Merritt, J. (n.d.). WHAT ARE MENTAL MODELS? Retrieved September 16, 2019, from https://thesystemsthinker.com/what-are-mental-models/.
36. Farnam Street. (n.d.). Understanding your Circle of Competence: How Warren Buffett Avoids Problems. Retrieved September 16, 2019, from https://fs.blog/2013/12/circle-of-competence/.

37. The Best Schools. (2018). The 100 Best Public High Schools in the U.S. Retrieved September 18, 2019, from https://thebestschools.org/rankings/best-public-high-schools-us/#top.
38. Shonk, K. (2019, May 9). 5 Common Negotiation Mistakes and How You Can Avoid Them. Retrieved September 26, 2019, from https://www.pon.harvard.edu/daily/negotiation-skills-daily/5-common-negotiation-mistakes-and-how-you-can-avoid-them/.
39. British Library. (n.d.). Robert Cialdini. Retrieved September 17, 2019, from https://www.bl.uk/people/robert-cialdini.
40. Poor Ash's Almanac. (n.d.). FISHER, URY, AND PATTON'S "GETTING TO YES": BOOK REVIEW, NOTES + ANALYSIS. Retrieved September 17, 2019, from http://www.askeladdencapital.com/fishe

r-ury-and-pattons-getting-to-yes-book-review/.

41. Poor Ash's Almanac. (n.d.). HUMANS VS. ECONS MENTAL MODEL. Retrieved September 17, 2019, from http://www.askeladdencapital.com/humans-vs-econs-mental-model/.

42. McVagh, A. (2018, May 23). Mental Model Summary: Reason Respecting (Because Why). Retrieved September 27, 2019, from https://www.mymentalmodels.info/mms-reason-respecting/.

www.ingramcontent.com/pod-product-compliance
Lightning Source LLC
Chambersburg PA
CBHW062037120526
44592CB00035B/1210